*To all those lay women and men
whose seriousness in faith
renews hope in the church
generation after generation.*

Becoming
a Thinking
Christian

JOHN B. COBB, Jr.

Abingdon Press
NASHVILLE

BECOMING A THINKING CHRISTIAN

Library of Congress Cataloging-in-Publication Data

Cobb, John B.
    Becoming a thinking Christian: if we want church renewal, we will
have to renew thinking in the church/John B. Cobb, Jr.
        p.   cm.
    ISBN 0-687-28752-9 (alk. paper)
    1. Theology, Doctrinal—Popular works. 2. Theology—Methodology.
3. Church renewal. 4. Church and the world. I. Title.
BT77.C56   1993
230'.044—dc20   93-14951
                                                                                   CIP

Scripture quotations are from the New Revised Standard Version Bible,
Copyright 1989 by the Division of Christian Education of the National Council of
the Churches of Christ in the USA. Used by permission.

04 05 06 07 08   ——   15 14 13 12 11

MANUFACTURED IN THE UNITED STATES OF AMERICA

CONTENTS

PREFACE

This book is for you if you are a committed lay Christian in one of the oldline Protestant churches. It invites you to become aware of the beliefs by which you live and to think about them. That means that it invites you to become aware that you are already a theologian and to become a good one.

To be a good theologian is to be a Christian who thinks. Thinking is hard. You cannot profit from this book without thinking.

Some suppose that there is a contradiction involved in this. Books for laypeople should be easy. That is wrong. Laypeople are just as capable of hard intellectual work as are professional theologians. Many laypeople have proven their intellectual prowess again and again in their chosen vocations (doctors, lawyers, managers, engineers, etc.). But most laity are not accustomed to *this* particular kind of thinking about *this* particular subject. Many very intelligent people are still operating out of a simplistic view of faith. Too many have been led to assume that faith is incompatible with intellectual challenge and integrity. They have stopped expecting the church to ask this of them. But that is the problem to which this book is addressed. It calls for thinking about that problem and thinking to overcome it. That is why it is a demanding book.

Still it is written for you as a layperson. That means that the thinking it calls for and talks about, and the way it talks about it, does not require the kinds of knowledge that only specialists are likely to have. It does refer to a few features of the Christian tradition that may not be familiar to you, but it explains them sufficiently for the purpose in ways that are not obscure.

The hard thinking it calls for is about yourself and your own beliefs. The subject is one you know well! The topics are familiar. What is hard is to *think* about them. The book cannot make that easy. Nothing can, except practice. If you read the book just for information about what I am saying, it may not be so hard. But then the book will fail. *The purpose of this book is to encourage you to think—as a Christian.*

The best way to encourage someone to think is to ask questions and interact with the answers. That is the method of dialogue, and dialogue in its finest form involves just two people. Your answer to one question determines what the next question should be. Unfortunately, a book cannot offer that kind of personal interaction. That means that a book is not the best way to help you. Long, sustained conversations would be far better. Thus this book encourages you to find conversation partners.

What most books do is to give you the ideas of the author. These are often excellent, and sometimes they stimulate you to think in new ways. But no amount of learning about the ideas of others takes the place of thinking *for yourself,* and the general stimulus of encountering new ideas usually does not go far toward making you think carefully and critically.

A book can do more to encourage you to think for yourself than just stimulate you with new ideas, and this one tries to do so. It can give examples of the sort of careful and critical thinking that can bring your Christian faith to bear on important issues. Some of these examples may connect with the way you think about the same matters. That may make it easier to get started on your own thinking. But these examples can only be suggestive.

In general, the arguments presented in this book are convincing to me, and in that sense you will learn, as in most books, what the author thinks. But that is not the main point here. The effort is to lay out arguments in ways that will enable you to agree or disagree at each step, and then to develop different arguments where you make different judgments. If the book succeeds, your thinking will take its own course; otherwise it will not be *your* thinking. Sometimes it will lead to conclusions that are quite different from those presented.

But if the book succeeds, you will not simply assert your disagreement with conclusions. You will make explicit the bases of your views and examine these bases with some care to see whether you find them Christian. That is hard, partly because the relation among ideas is not easy to clarify, but also because we do not like to question beliefs that we have held, sometimes for a long time.

The book also contains some abstract talk about why it is important that you, as a lay Christian, think, how you can get started, some steps your thinking may take, what sources you may need to draw on, and where all this may take you. To understand what you have not previously thought about is also a kind of thinking that is demanding.

You can become a better theologian than many of the professionals! That is because becoming a professional theologian is more a matter of thinking about other people's beliefs than about one's own. This book will try to clarify the difference. If you become serious about being a theologian, at times you will need help from the professionals—maybe a lot of help. But you will not expect them to do your thinking for you! Real Christian theology is not a matter for professionals. It is for Christians who think. Professionals may do that, too. But that is because they are Christians who think, not because they have the specialized knowledge that makes them professionals.

I will be pleased if pastors realize that their needs are much the same. They, too, are part of the *laos,* the people of God, and they are not professional scholars. There is no guarantee that their theological education turned them into good theologians. It may have introduced them to the various disciplines of their teachers. It may have encouraged thinking about how to respond to some of the problems of leading a congregation and serving its people. It may have informed them about the theologies of important thinkers in past and present. But it may not have encouraged them to think very much about their own beliefs. If they have not acquired the habit of thinking on that topic, then this book is for them, too.

9

It won't hurt professional theologians to listen in. Sometimes professionals suppose that lay Christians become theologians by being introduced to the academic disciplines of the professionals. Indeed, too many Christians have bought into that idea of what a theologian is. They know they don't have time or inclination to go far down that road; so they leave theology to the experts. The consequences for individual Christians and for the church are disastrous. If we want church renewal, we will have to renew thinking in the church.

In fact, if there is a renewal of thinking in the church, there *will* be church renewal. Without it, there won't. Trying to renew the church with gimmicks, or merely by arousing emotion, will not do the job. The church is strong only when it lives by the mature convictions of its members. Mature convictions are shaped in thought.

I have been thinking for some time about the separation of what is called theology—what I as a professional theologian have been doing—and the life of the church and its members. The separation has seemed to me, increasingly, to be disastrous for both. I have been complaining about it, writing about it, and lecturing about it. In one sense this book comes out of that thinking.

But in another sense it is specifically and directly a response to an invitation by Rex Matthews, Abingdon Press editor. He sensed a need and wanted me to address it. Step by step in conversation with him I began to understand what he wanted. This book is not exactly what he wanted, but what relevance it has is owed to a large extent to him. I have never before written a book so much in response to another's perceptions of what is needed. I am grateful to Rex for his insight, his perseverance, his encouragement, and his guidance.

CHAPTER ONE

On Becoming What You Are

A THEOLOGIAN

1. Reclaiming Authority from the Professionals

We live in an age of professionalism. Some of the professions have been around a long time. We have had lawyers to do legal work, doctors to take care of our health, teachers to educate our children for generations. In more recent times we have developed more professions: economists to explain and manage the economy, engineers to make and run our elaborate technology, and managers to order our organizations. We have morticians and beauticians, psychotherapists and dieticians, agronomists and journalists, and on and on and on.

Much of this is inescapable and desirable. Much more expertise is brought to bear on the varied functions of society. But there are also problems. We become dependent on others even with respect to things that we could do for ourselves. We turn to experts in everything except what we are expert in ourselves. No one seems to have the whole picture, to know how all the parts fit together. Many jobs get done better through this specialization, but as human beings we are in some way diminished. We take less responsibility for who and what we are.

This book is about a particular manifestation of this general problem. Theologians have also been for a long time a profession. But most Christians have known that they could not leave theology to the theologians. Christians have to do their believing for themselves, and believing is a theological act.

There have been times when Christian laypeople were very

much aware of this. There was lively discussion in the churches of what it meant to believe and of what the right beliefs were. For a while Protestant churches in particular were quite successful in encouraging their members to take responsibility for their own beliefs. But in the nineteenth century professional theology began to grow separate from the life of laypeople. In the second half of the twentieth century the situation has become worse. It has reached crisis proportions in the oldline denominations in the United States.

This crisis is less often recognized than others. The oldline churches are declining, and they look around for reasons. One of them stares us in the eyes, but is rarely mentioned: Many of us have stopped taking responsibility for our own theology. *Theology* has come to mean something done only by professionals, and only a few Christians are attracted to that profession.

The church could live with a change in the way things are named. *Theology* could mean what a few professors do, if other Christians continued to talk seriously about faith under another label. But that is not happening. In most congregations there is little serious talk about what faith is and what lay Christians really do believe.

Theology has been professionalized, and when any activity is professionalized, those who are not professionals are intimidated by the expertise of those who are. We expect them to take care of things, and we do not even ask for an explanation. Or if we hear an explanation that does not make sense to us, we shrug our shoulders. We assume the experts know what they are talking about, even if we don't.

That is an exaggeration, of course. Every now and again one of our experts says something we don't like, and we take offense. Sometimes we don't trust a doctor's advice, and we seek a "second opinion." We laugh about how one can hire an "expert witness" to testify to almost anything. We ask how we can have any idea of what to do when even the experts disagree. Often even our recognition that professionals may not know as much as they are supposed to know tends more to reduce our responsibility than to heighten it.

There are, nevertheless, a few areas in which we are taking back some responsibility for our lives. Health care is one. We continue to depend on medical doctors for many things, but more of us are trying to understand enough about health so that we are not mindlessly following doctors' orders. We study diet—aided by professionals there, too—but learn to evaluate the various ideas in relation to our experience. The same is true of exercise. Millions find help in remedies that are not recognized in orthodox medicine at all. In other words, we are resuming basic responsibility for our health, learning how to make use of professional expertise, rather than simply depending on authority.

Something like that is happening religiously too. More and more of us have become interested in spirituality. That can mean a lot of things. But in general it means that we sense a need to order and deepen our inner lives, and we no longer look to institutions or experts to tell us how to do it. We search for the teachers who can help us learn, and we develop our own way of being.

2. Reclaiming Theology from Professional Theologians

It is time for the same thing to happen with theology. It is time for all Christians to take responsibility for their personal beliefs. Professionals can help, but believing is something each Christian must do for herself or himself.

The problem has not been that lay Christians have let the professionals think for them. They have not blindly adopted the conclusions of the professionals. On the contrary, too many Christians have not even bothered to ask what these conclusions were. They have simply let the professionals do their thing, supposing it must have some importance for someone, and must therefore be done. Occasionally some question has arisen on which professional opinion is needed. Usually the professionals disagree, and laypeople are confirmed in the view that theology is beyond their competence and none of their business. When professionals do speak on subjects that touch the whole community quite directly, often what they say is disturbing. This sometimes stirs up a flurry of discussion.

One such flurry was caused in the mid-sixties by the proclamation that God is dead. In professional circles this is not a

13

new idea. Friedrich Nietzsche in the late nineteenth century asserted the death of God, and professional philosophers and theologians have responded in many ways. But the vigorous renewal of this discussion in the 1960s attracted the attention of the secular press. And through that channel, especially *Time* magazine, church people became involved. Unfortunately, church leadership in general failed to use the occasion to stimulate theological discussion throughout the church. Instead, it tried to douse the flames and reassure the faithful.

More recently, "the Jesus seminar" has evoked some attention. Again, it is primarily through the secular press that lay Christians have learned about what is going on. In this case, a group of reputable scholars is trying to come to consensus on the question of which sayings attributed to Jesus in the four Gospels are authentic—that is, the actual words spoken by the historical Jesus. Since most professional New Testament scholars emphasize the role of the early Christian community in shaping the Gospels, the results are often shocking to those who have not been aware of this feature of historical scholarship. To learn from the newspaper that scholars deny that Jesus actually said much of what is placed on his lips in the New Testament has been upsetting to many. There has been an opportunity to stimulate discussion. But the churches have not seized this opportunity.

There is a reason that not much is happening. Theology is controversial. Christians have never all held the same beliefs, and when we dig into beliefs, we discover that they are important. How, then, can we get along with people with whom we disagree? How can we work together?

Those with institutional responsibility want harmony rather than controversy. Most laypeople did not learn about the death of God controversy or the results of the Jesus seminar through their churches. On the whole, the role of church leadership was to assure them that they need not concern themselves with such matters. Sometimes it seems that church leaders prefer that the church die in superficial harmony than live in vigorous debate.

This way of putting matters is unfair to the church's leadership. The truth is that the shock of confrontation with what professional theologians are doing and saying is not the best way for theological discussion to emerge in the church. Theology is controversial, and controversy is not to be avoided. But as Christians, we need to learn what theology is, to take responsibility for our own theology on other grounds. The failure of the church is not that it smoothed over sensational challenges to popular belief. The real failure is that it does not encourage wide participation in theological reflection.

This book is not addressed to the institution. Even if the institutional church does not encourage you to take responsibility for your beliefs, you can still do so. This is what happened with respect to spirituality. People found their spiritual needs were not being met in the ordinary life of the church, and they searched for programs and literature that would be more helpful. And they found that help. Some of them brought what they found back into the church. On the other hand, some people left the church altogether, because they found more help elsewhere. The church pays a huge price for neglecting the deeper needs of its people.

3. The Theology of Spirituality

One reason why theological discussion is so important is that every spirituality involves a theology. It is possible to adopt a spirituality on a quite pragmatic basis. It seems to help some of us in daily life, or it gives glimpses of a dimension otherwise missing, or it quiets a deep inner restlessness. That is all fine. But it is better to know what we are doing.

An example will help to show the problem. Not long ago there was a lot of interest in this country in Transcendental Meditation. It provided a simple discipline that had demonstratively positive results. Some public schools introduced it as a way to improve attitudes and learning in the classroom. It worked. The leaders insisted it was not a religion but a discipline that anyone could adopt.

However, this was not quite true. Transcendental Meditation was developed out of Hindu spiritual practices, and there was an elaborate theory behind it. People could practice some simple disciplines in ignorance of the theory. But if they were drawn into a deeper involvement, the practice into which they would enter was more and more specifically Hindu.

15

That is not, of itself, a reason for us to reject Transcendental Meditation. The history of Christianity is one of borrowing from other communities and integrating what is borrowed into the life of the church. But this process works better when we know what we are doing, and that involves theology. Unfortunately, the lay quest for spirituality, hopeful and encouraging as it is, has taken place in a time when most of us think very little about theology.

Equally important is the question of whether Protestants should seek spirituality at all. The word *spirituality* comes from the Latin *spiritualitas,* which refers to the quality of life sought in the monasteries through ascetic disciplines. It was associated with a sense of superiority on the part of those who separated from the world and lived the "religious" life. Martin Luther rejected this whole pattern. He taught that the Christian needs faith, not spirituality, that the Christian life is to be lived in the world and not in separation from it. Faith expresses itself in discipleship, not in the cultivation of special inner states.

We might reply that these old debates from Reformation times have nothing to do with what Protestants are seeking as spirituality today. That may or may not be true. More likely it is true in some instances and not in others. Furthermore, if contemporary spirituality does participate in what Luther opposed, that may be no reason to oppose it today. Luther may have been wrong, or the dangers of that day may no longer be present today. But we cannot be sure that there is no problem. We should not blindly enter into something so important to our lives. In short, we need to consider the commitments and beliefs that are involved in seeking a spirituality at all as well as in the selection of one over another. We cannot avoid theological issues by turning to spirituality.

4. All Christians Are Already Theologians

Up to now the argument has been that all believers need, and need urgently, to reclaim responsibility for our beliefs. That means we should become theologians. But how can we do that? Must we turn to the difficult writings of the professionals and accept their conclusions? Clearly, that won't work. That is not the way we have begun to reclaim responsibility for our physical

16

health. We rarely study the textbooks used in medical schools. To take responsibility is to *use* the expertise of others, but to use it selectively in the context of a wider perspective than is our own.

But how can we gain that wider perspective? If we are not already theologians, how can we become theologians except by accepting ideas on the authority of others?

The answer is that *all Christians already are theologians.* The call to take responsibility for belief is not a call to generate beliefs out of nothing. It is a call to become responsible, first of all, with regard to beliefs already in place. We need to become what we are! That is, we need to do with increasing responsibility what we are already inevitably doing.

The analogy of taking responsibility for bodily health can be carried one more step. There has never been a time when people have not engaged in activities that affected their health. They have eaten and slept and exercised in one way or another. Indeed, in the past they often medicated themselves as well. There was a lot of folk wisdom about how to take care of the body.

With the rise of modern medicine, however, people became skeptical of home remedies, and they paid less attention to how the way they lived affected their health. When they got sick, instead of going to bed and taking home remedies, they went to the doctor for a shot of penicillin. They placed themselves in the hands of the professional expert, and they thought of medicine as the answer to problems of health. They thought it was the doctor's responsibility to take care of them, and they paid less attention to the things they could do for themselves.

Now that is being reversed. We view personal health more inclusively. We see that medical specialists contribute to health in important, but limited, ways. We make decisions about when we need assistance and who is best qualified to provide it. We can do a great deal to reduce our need for professional expertise. We learn from many sources what makes for health, but we form integrated conclusions based on our experiences. In the process, we talk with one another about what we have found beneficial more than we talk with the experts. More and more of us are taking responsibility for health care back into our own hands.

There is some similarity with theology. People have always had ideas about their health that affected how they behaved. They did not have to develop such ideas out of nothing, but they did need to become aware of what these ideas were and change and develop them. Similarly with theology, Christians have always had beliefs that influenced their lives. We do not need to develop such ideas out of nothing, but we do need to become aware of these beliefs and to change and develop them as life experience and reflection lead us to do so.

So there *is* a place to begin in the process of becoming what we already are. That is, all of us are already theologians in the sense that we do have beliefs that affect our Christian lives. But affirming this fact is just a beginning.

The main problem is that in the oldline Protestant denominations, most of us are very diffident about these beliefs. We hold our beliefs doubtfully and insecurely. We are not sure what the doctrines to which we acquiesce mean, and when the teachings are explained, we are often still less sure that we really believe them. One reason why theological discussion rarely takes hold among laypeople in oldline churches is that it often focuses on these doubtful beliefs. Many of us are unsure of ourselves in talking about theology, and, in fact, it does not seem to make a lot of difference anyway.

Taking responsibility for our theology cannot mean that we talk more about our confused opinions on traditional questions whose importance is unclear. That won't work. Instead, it must mean discovering and articulating the convictions that really shape our lives. That requires a quite different starting point. It requires also a kind of reflection to which most people are not accustomed.

We are likely to be intimidated by the proposal that we need to think in new ways. We suppose that will require a special expertise, and we doubt our ability to acquire it. We prefer that some special group—one made up of *other* people—do this thinking. That is the resistance that this book wants to break down. The kind of thinking that is needed is different, but not inaccessible. You can engage in it. To some limited extent, you already do. You just need to pay more attention and to commit yourself to some hard work.

Where can we best begin to become more aware of the convictions that already shape our lives? No one place is best for everyone. Christians are individuals with distinct interests and emphases. The ideal would be to think through with each individual how best to get started. But that cannot be done in a book. The best that can be done here is to start in areas in which many of us can realize that we do have convictions.

To avoid the impression that there is some one place for everyone to begin, I conclude this chapter with three examples taken from the ordinary life of the church. These illustrate ways in which our theological ideas affect us and show how we can become more conscious of what our beliefs are. These three examples are about tragedy, prayer, and feminism.

5. Two Responses to Tragedy

The death of a loved one is a time when basic beliefs come to the surface. And these beliefs affect the way we minister to the bereaved. Laypeople often share this ministry of comfort with pastors. What do you say to one who has lost a spouse or child?

There is a tragic element in every death, but more acute theological issues are raised when the death is untimely. Each situation is different, but there are some commonalities, and there is likely to be some consistency in the way you try to comfort those who have suffered this kind of loss.

Of course, some of what you say may be purely conventional and this cannot be used as a basis for exploring your real beliefs. But that is not true of all that you say. Sometimes your deep convictions are expressed in confrontation with death. Let's consider two approaches of consoling parents whose son has died of leukemia, with which you may or may not identify.

Pauline Simmons encourages the parents to accept the death of their child. She believes that, despite all appearances, what happened is for the best. God would not have let the child have leukemia or taken his life if there had not been a reason. We *may* be able to get some glimmer of what this reason is, but that is not necessary.

She accepts by faith that there *is* a reason, and she tries to help the bereaved parents accept this, too.

The belief about God that underlies Simmons's way of counseling the bereaved is that whatever happens in the world

19

expresses God's purpose. That is because God is all powerful, or at least decisively powerful over all. The appearance of an accident or of the victory of evil over good is an illusion. Since God is ultimately responsible for all that happens, Simmons is sure that the appearance that chance or sin is in control is only that—an appearance.

What appears evil is finally for the good. Indeed, this is close to the heart of what faith is for her. The fact that all life is in God's hand means that evil cannot triumph. Thus the appearance of the triumph of evil is an illusion. She is confident that in the end all will be well.

David Chen responds to this tragedy in a different way. He tells the parents that the leukemia and death of the boy are truly evil, an evil that God did not want or intend. God wants the good, and that means life and health, not disease or untimely death. God is with the bereaved, suffering with them. The comfort comes from the belief in this presence and sharing. The right response, according to Chen, is not to accept the evil as if it were good, but to work in the world so that this kind of evil will not occur again.

Chen has a very different view of God and the world from that of Simmons. God does not cause each thing to happen as it does. God works for good and works with us against evil. Human beings have real freedom, and they often use that freedom badly. Many of the evils of life result from this misuse of freedom either from ignorance or from sin. Also, chance plays a role. Many events are against God's will and should not be accepted as if they were ultimately good.

6. Two Views of Prayer

Most of us pray, although the extent of our praying, the sense of its importance, the reasons for praying, and what we pray for vary greatly. Examination of whether, why, and how we pray can be quite revealing of our theologies.

Consider, first, Fred Gaspari, who prays only in a perfunctory way in order to fit in with the rest of the congregation. He bows his head and closes his eyes in church when expected to do so. But he does not see that the form of prayer is really appropriate. This is particularly true for him with regard to prayers of petition and intercession.

Gaspari is neither an agnostic nor an atheist. He is a serious Christian who believes strongly in God. His skepticism about the value of petitionary and intercessory prayer expresses particular views of God that he is prepared to articulate as part of his Christian theology.

He believes that the world in which we live witnesses to a Creator; that the world is very good, so that we have every reason to praise this Creator; that the Creator established moral as well as natural laws, so that it is incumbent on us to obey them; and that the Creator will also be our judge at death. He believes, however, that the Creator does not intervene in the creation. The Creator has given us the freedom and responsibility to live morally, and what happens to us and to others depends on whether we do that. Asking God to intervene to accomplish what God has left for us to do is at best pointless, at worst, wrong.

As a second example, consider Edith Gutowski, for whom the life of prayer is central to her Christian being. Her prayer expresses gratitude not only for creation and life in general, but also for specific occurrences each day. It includes expressions of penitence and requests for forgiveness. It gives her a strong sense of God's guiding presence, and it includes requests for herself and for others: prayers for peace, for healing, for strengthening in faith, and sometimes for quite specific goods.

It is obvious that Gutowski's understanding of God and the world is different from that of Gaspari. Like him she believes that God is creator of all and has given a moral as well as a natural law. She, too, believes in God's final judgment. But these beliefs do not come to expression centrally in her prayers. Instead, the operative belief is that God is intimately related to the details of the world.

It would be going too far to say that her prayer life supposes that God is the cause of everything that happens. But it does imply that God is influential in the course of events. She also believes, at least implicitly, that her praying has some effect on the character and extent of God's influence. That means that she thinks in terms of a certain interaction between creatures and God.

7. Feminism and God

In concluding this chapter, we will discuss another topic at greater length. This is taken from a current controversy that is important nationally and in some congregations: debates related to the gender of God. Consider a possible scenario in a local church.

A women's group studies feminist issues and becomes aware of the masculine bias of the Sunday morning liturgy. The group decides that this bias is distorting for the church in general and for them in particular. For example, the fact that the worship service consistently refers to God in male terms devalues the feminine aspect of reality. The women discuss what they should do and decide that the use of terms referring to gender should be reduced, but not eliminated. Instead of eliminating them, the liturgy should balance the use of masculine and feminine terms. God can be spoken of sometimes as Father and as King. But there should be an equal use of feminine language, such as Mother and Queen.

The women go to the worship committee. Some members of that committee agree with them. Others are shocked and view the proposal as blasphemous. The argument focuses on whether God can rightly be called Mother and Queen.

Obviously, much of the negative reaction comes out of shock. Many people do not like being asked to change. They just want things left as they are. It is possible to give theological reasons for avoiding change, but the psychological factor probably dominates.

Let us suppose, however, that some of those who oppose this change do not oppose change in general. They have led in innovations. For them the objection has to do with their understanding of God and of the relation of God to biblical images.

One extreme possibility is that some of them really do believe that God is male. However, that can be set aside if "male" includes the physical characteristics of the human male. The issue is not about genitalia. The issue is about the divine character. Some believe that God relates to us like a human father rather than like a human mother. For example, the giving of law and judgment

22

is more properly associated with a father than with a mother. This does not exclude mercy and forgiveness, but the mercy and forgiveness are from the one whose laws have been broken, and they have a fatherly character. Hence, although God is not biologically male, God relates to us as a father rather than as a mother. In this sense, God is masculine, even though "he" is not a male.

In reply the women may argue that this is exactly what troubles them with leaving the patriarchal language intact. It confirms in the worshiper the sense that only the masculine characteristics are divine. That cannot avoid giving the impression that masculine characteristics are superior to feminine ones. And that, in turn, inevitably undergirds a patriarchal society in which women's place is to support men rather than to play an independent and equal role in shaping public life. With this value system unchallenged, only those women who take on masculine characteristics can play this public role.

The response of those who resist the change in language may be that these are interesting pragmatic considerations, but such considerations cannot decide the question of what God is actually like. That must be learned from the Bible. There God is depicted as creating the world from without, a male image, rather than giving birth to the world in a motherly way. God is depicted as lawgiver and judge. God is revealed in Jesus, a male. And Jesus consistently addresses God as "Father." Christians cannot ignore all that and simply reinvent the object of their worship!

The women may reply that through Christian history it has been emphasized that God is far beyond all that we can think and imagine. No image of God is true. All images are pointers to something that is so different from us that it cannot really be spoken at all. To be attached to particular images is, therefore, a form of idolatry. There is no question but that through biblical times and through the history of the church, masculine images have dominated overwhelmingly. That is just the problem. We are now able to see how one-sided all of this has been.

Furthermore, what is remarkable in the New Testament is not that Jesus was a man. If God had been incarnate in a woman, no one would ever have known about that. What is remarkable is that the revelation in Jesus balances masculine and feminine characteristics in God so well. It is the church that has destroyed that balance. If we really believe that it is in Jesus that we come to know God, it is appropriate to highlight the feminine aspects of God alongside the masculine.

Much is at stake in this debate, and very deep theological assumptions come to expression in it. One issue is the actual character of God. Do we believe that God has more masculine than feminine characteristics? Certainly there are extensive arguments for that from Scripture and tradition. Hence, if we attribute straightforward authority to these, we have a good reason for supposing that God really *is* masculine, so that a change of language would simply falsify the reality.

Even the philosophical theology that undergirds the women's argument that God is wholly beyond gender differentiation nevertheless presents God in male terms. It describes God as wholly self-sufficient, active, impassible, and immutable. As we examine these ideas, we can see that they represent ideals associated historically with masculinity. They do not express the way we would think of an ideal mother.

The women's argument requires that both Scripture and tradition be used against themselves. They are both patriarchal through and through. But they both include principles of self-criticism that offer leverage. We can argue that although the prophetic movement was male and did not challenge patriarchy, its call for justice, its conviction that God was on the side of the oppressed, and its willingness to challenge existing structures, both religious and secular, provide the basis for identifying other oppressions and asserting that in those cases, too, God sides with the oppressed. Similarly, there is a strong criticism of idolatry in the Bible, so that if we can show that its own teaching is not free of idolatrous elements, then it is appropriate for those who claim the heritage of the Bible to criticize features of its dominant message.

Of all forms of Christian theology today, feminist theology is under the most pressure to radicalize the authority of the Bible in this way. The question is whether this kind of radicalization is what being Christian today demands, or whether this is a compromise that subordinates Christian identity to something else. This is an issue for some Christian feminists themselves.

The resistance to change in the church is so deep that some

feminists decide that the members of the worship committee who oppose them are correct, that the God of Christianity really *is* masculine, and that, therefore, to be a Christian is to exalt masculinity above femininity. On the basis of accepting the accuracy of the arguments of those who resist change, they find that they must consider themselves post-Christian, since their own deepest conviction is that God does not side against them in their struggle for the liberation of women. The future shape of the church will be deeply affected by its decision to commit itself to patriarchy or to open itself to feminist concerns.

DOING YOUR THEOLOGY

You can, of course, turn to chapter 2 and read on. However, you will lose most of the potential value of this book if you do so. You will not discover what your own beliefs are or improve them without *thinking*—and thinking takes time.

You can respond to the following questions and proposals in two ways. If you are working on this alone, you can *write*. If you are working with others, you can *talk*. A combination is better still. If two or more people work together, and if each writes first, and then there is discussion of what has been written, progress can be rapid. Best of all is to write again after the discussion.

This proposal will work best if you have strong views on the topic you treat. Hence, you should make your selections accordingly. However, if you are unsure on all topics, you can still proceed by clarifying your uncertainty and testing alternative hypotheses.

The questions are written on the assumption that your primary identity is as a Christian and that you intend to think about all these matters as a Christian. The task is then to fulfill this intention. If this does not apply to you, then the exercises will not work for you as written. It will still be worthwhile to clarify how you see the relation between being a Christian and the way you think about various matters.

The divided identity that is so common today—between being a Christian, say, and being a biologist or a feminist or a capitalist—is discussed more in chapter 4, especially section two. If you recognize yourself in this divided identity, but have some desire to attain a more unified way of being, you may want to read that chapter before trying to write. But if you are committed to being a Christian, you should start writing and talking now!

1. Consider how you comfort bereaved parents, your prayer life, or how you view changing gender language about God. Are your views similar to any of those described in this chapter?
   Select one of these topics and formulate your position in agreement or contrast with those described.
2. Reflect on the assumptions underlying this position, especially the beliefs about God that come to expression in your position. For example, does your position presuppose that
   a. what we do affects God?
   b. prayer affects what happens in the world?
   c. God is all-powerful?
   d. everything that happens is in accordance with God's will?
   e. what appears evil is ultimately for the best?
   f. God guarantees a positive outcome at the end?
   g. God acts independently as well as through creatures?
   h. God's relation to us is more like that of a father than of a mother?
   i. biblical language and imagery should always be retained?
3. Justify your beliefs. What role does Scripture play in their justification?
4. Select another topic and repeat this procedure. Possible topics are worship with non-Christians, tithing, displaying the national flag in church, the church's taking stands on controversial political issues, killing animals for human food.

CHAPTER TWO

Ethics and Theology

1. Introduction

To be a Christian is to try to live a Christian life. There are competing ideas about just what that life should be. We have noticed that there are different opinions about spirituality, for example. But all agree that one important part of a Christian life is morality. Also, this aspect of the Christian life is resistant to being professionalized. We Christians have to make moral decisions individually for ourselves. We can seek help and guidance from others, but the decisions are our own, and if the decisions are poor, we bear the consequences.

We can live without thinking much about what we believe. We can live without consciously adopting a spirituality. But life forces decisions on us, and many of these decisions have a moral character. Most of us feel we are able to make reasonable judgments about what is right and what is wrong, even if we know that we sometimes do wrong. About some of these matters, at least, most Christians have strong convictions.

There are many starting places in ordinary church life for becoming clearer *that* we have convictions and *what* these convictions are; we noted several of these places in chapter 1. But it may be that issues of morality have special importance to many of us and are especially good places to pursue the task of becoming better theologians.

In this chapter, we will consider some of these issues in much the same way we dealt with the topics of chapter 1. But as we proceed we will also pursue the analysis a bit further. We want not only to become clear as to what our convictions are but also to think more systematically and self-critically about them.

2. Abortion

A heated national debate has brought the relation of morality to theology to the fore. Abortion is certainly a moral issue. But the debate, even outside the church, cannot escape a theological cast. Yet most people are not willing to leave it to theologians to resolve. They have their own convictions.

One of the reasons why the theological character of the debate is so clear is that there is no explicit teaching about abortion in the Bible. That may sound strange, since some people almost identify theology with biblical proof texts. Using biblical passages as proof texts does express a particular theological position—namely that the Bible is literally inerrant and that every statement applies to us now regardless of the context and purpose in which it was originally formulated. As long as those who hold these two beliefs can find the relevant proof texts, they do not need any other Christian convictions. They can avoid having to think.

On many other issues, this works for them. They can thus escape any further need for theological reflection. But on the issue of abortion they cannot. On the basis of biblical texts, they can certainly affirm that innocent people are not to be killed. But they cannot, on the basis of such texts alone, decide whether a fetus is a person. The only biblical passage that comes close to discussing this topic (Exod. 21:22-25) tends to imply that it is not.

But even among those who incline toward looking for proof texts, few regard the passage in Exodus as decisive. They are forced to turn to other arguments, such as those developed in the later tradition. This draws them into a more complex theological discussion.

In the early centuries of the Christian tradition, the debate was over when the human soul appeared in the fetus. The position of Saint Augustine was that once the soul was there, the killing of the fetus would be murder; prior to that, it was not such a serious matter. Contemporary philosophers sometimes argue similarly that the issue is whether the mind has come into existence. The

28

Roman Catholic position today, on the other hand, is that no sharp line can be drawn, so that the fetus must be considered a person from conception. Others who agree that no sharp line can be drawn argue that this means that the fetus only gradually becomes a human person.

If we adopt the Roman Catholic view that it is wrong to kill a fertilized ovum, what will we say about forcing a woman to bring an unwanted fetus to term? Does a woman have any right to decide what happens within her own body? How does such a right relate to the right of the fetus to live?

The debate keeps circling around the understanding of the human being. What makes a human being one of those especially precious creatures for whom God cares so much? Is it membership in the biological species? Is it the potential to become a person? Or is it the realization of that potential through the care of other people in community?

Abortion is a good example of how a moral issue brings to the fore particular theological ideas. In this case, these ideas have to do chiefly with the question of what constitutes a person. Abortion also raises the issue of women's rights. Christians who make judgments about the morality of abortion can examine the beliefs that come to expression in these judgments. This is another example of how to become aware of what our theological beliefs are.

3. Questions About Money

Consider how another set of issues can arise in the church. Let us suppose that a pastor, Philip Stewart, preaches on a biblical text that denounces the pursuit of wealth at the expense of the poor, and that a businessman, Roger Schwartz, becomes angry. Schwartz believes that his anger is justified, that he has thought through these matters, and that the preacher has no business condemning him in this way.

Roger's objection is that the Bible is quite naive about economics. He believes the church should acknowledge its limitations and allow the experts in this field to determine what is to be thought about profits and wealth. On the whole, the church does this in physics and biology. Why does it think it has the right to meddle in economics?

Christianity, he believes, has its proper sphere, dealing, especially, with personal morality and specifically religious questions. It may also be able to speak about the family and other more intimate aspects of life. But it is not equipped to deal with the public world, and when Christians claim to do this as Christians, they are out of place. Being Christian does not give one the necessary knowledge.

Schwartz knows that this view has implications for biblical authority. It implies that the Bible has authority only in matters of faith and personal morality. This leads to a quite selective reading. He suspects that it has implications also for the understanding of God and of how God is known and about God's concern for people. He sees that it might sound as though he thinks God cares only about faith and personal morality. But in fact his position is that although God cares about the whole, the revelation in the Bible is only about these special matters.

According to this theology, the way God's purposes are to be realized in other respects is to be learned from those who are expert in the relevant fields—in this case, economists. From them Christians learn that God's purposes are best attained when each person pursues his or her private economic interests, and that means profit, as vigorously as possible. In that way the whole economy grows. Of course, this was not understood in Jesus' day any more than quantum theory was understood then. To derive economic theory from the Bible is as foolish as to derive physics there. The vigorous pursuit of individual advantage in the market differs from the way God wants people to act in the family, in the church, and with friends. In that more intimate area, the understanding of what is needed in Jesus' day can apply unchanged.

Schwartz's views have implications in other areas about which he has not thought much. If biblical teachings are authoritative only in areas in which there is no new, reliable knowledge from other sources, then biblical teachings on sexuality, for example, may have to be set aside along with those on economics. If he is not ready to agree on this, then he will need to think more deeply what his real beliefs are.

Peggy Ray, another businessperson in the congregation, is angered by the same sermon for other reasons. It made her feel guilty, and she is angry for being forced to confront what she believes to be her real sin. Her underlying theological beliefs are quite different from those of Schwartz. She is deeply convinced of the wisdom of the biblical suspicion of the pursuit of gain, and yet she finds no alternative in her workaday life. This leads her to the view that this world is too evil a place for the true morality of the gospel to be applied except by saints. She wishes she were a saint, and she tries to deemphasize the conflict between her business life and her Christian aspiration. She resents being forced to deal with it again. But she is not prepared to justify her resentment. Instead, she acknowledges that the resentment is also sinful.

4. God and Morality: Four Views

In addition to the theological convictions that come to expression in response to particular ethical issues, there is the question of the basis of morality as a whole. Much moral teaching seems to be a simple matter of common sense and hardly raises fundamental questions. But what seems common sense to people in one culture does not always appear so to those who come from other cultural and religious backgrounds.

Furthermore, some philosophers have found that they cannot ground any objective morality in their philosophical beliefs and principles. Some go so far as to say that right and wrong are simply a matter of taste. Christians do not agree, and this leads to the recognition that the way we think about morality is connected to the way we think about God.

One group of Christians thinks that morality is obedience to a moral law given by God. Therefore, obedience to that law is obedience to God. Some hold that law to be fully rational, open to all. Traditional natural law theory fits this pattern. It provides the basis of all morality, but many aspects of life are not thought of as bound by it. For example, many decisions about what to eat and drink and how to observe the Sabbath are somewhat disconnected from morality. Also, the moral law does not settle all issues simply. We have to use reason not only to discern what the law is but to see how to apply it in complex cases. The abortion debate is an example of this.

A second group thinks of the law as being far more detailed. The fact that it is not rationally evident that an act is wrong is not important if God has forbidden that act. God's command sets aside rational considerations. God has commanded many things that cannot be independently shown to be required by reason. Those who look for proof texts for their solutions to moral questions are thinking of moral law in this way.

Other Christians believe that law is not the right basis for Christian morality. The Christian is called to love God wholeheartedly and to act out of that love. Then the question is over what constitutes right service to God. Of course, many of the same actions follow from this understanding as from the others. But the theological position is different, and sometimes the ethical implications differ as well.

There is a further distinction here. Some, we will call this the third group, see service to God and service to other creatures as leading in different directions. Yet others, the fourth group, believe that people can serve God only in and through service of other creatures. The third group emphasizes specifically religious acts. The fourth group is more concerned with action in the world. In neither case will ethical decisions be made simply from quoting an ancient teaching. The Christian asks what, now, under present conditions, best serves God.

5. Applying the Four Views to Homosexuality

The differences in ethical judgments that follow from these different views of the relation of morality to God come out in another ethical debate, that about homosexuality. The issue is whether homosexual acts are, in and of themselves, sinful under all circumstances. When Christians who find themselves opposed to all homosexual acts as immoral examine the basis of their opposition, they often find that they are participating in one of the groups described above.

Sometimes they find themselves arguing from something like natural law theory. The argument, very simply, is that sexuality has a purpose—namely, procreation. Participation in sexual acts that cannot serve that purpose are against the law. This is God's law, written into the nature of things, and it is there to be discerned by all who consider sexuality objectively.

The second group thinks of the moral law as what God has declared regardless of its independent accessibility to our reason. They argue that the wrongness of homosexuality is explicitly stated in God's Word in several places. For them, no other argument or explanation is needed.

Members of the third group may also argue against homosexuality. They may hold that any who can do so should keep themselves free from worldly entanglements so as to devote themselves wholly to God. It is, of course, important that some, indeed many, marry and have families, so that the human race and the Christian community will continue. But for those to whom this door is closed, there is all the more reason to devote themselves solely to God.

Those Christians who find themselves denying that homosexual acts are necessarily forbidden to Christians are likely to belong to the fourth group described above. They understand that morality is the service of God, but they believe God is served in and through service of the creatures. The question for them is the effect of any sexual acts, heterosexual or homosexual, on human beings, both on those who take part and on others. If the quality of life generated by particular homosexual relations is superior to that which follows from sexual self-denial, then more is contributed to God through certain expressions of homosexual love than through suppressing it entirely.

Although there is a tendency for positions on this subject to line up in this way, the relation between a general theological conviction and specific ethical conclusions is rarely so simple. Among those who hold to any one of these four types of relations between God and morality, some will adopt the opposite conclusion. That reflects additional theological convictions.

Among those who believe that rightness and wrongness are written into the nature of things and accept natural law theory, some argue that sexuality has functions other than procreation alone, such as human intimacy, enjoyment, and mutual bonding.

They may even argue that today these functions have become more important than procreation. If so, then homosexual acts that promote intimacy, provide enjoyment, and lead to stable bonding are to be affirmed as good.

Against those who denounce all homosexual acts on the basis of a few biblical texts, it is possible to debate the original meaning of the texts. One can show that sometimes the translations from Hebrew and Greek are not quite accurate, so that the original does not directly address homosexuality. Or one may argue that the texts belong to a part of the Jewish law that is superseded by the gospel.

Against those who derive the superiority of celibacy from the separate service of God, it is possible to assert with Paul that even though such separation from the world is ideal, still it is better to marry than to burn. They can point out that homosexuals "burn," in the sense of being preoccupied with sexual feelings, no less than heterosexuals, and that it is better for them to find a wholesome outlet for their feelings than to try unsuccessfully to repress them.

In reverse, against those who hold that some homosexual practice contributes to human happiness and well-being, and thus also to God, one can argue that such practice in fact does more harm than good, causing more suffering than joy. If it is socially accepted, it weakens the fabric of society through undermining the institutions of marriage and family. If it is not socially acceptable, then the practice requires all kinds of secrecy and deception or invites hostility and persecution.

All of these debates continue. At this point in the book they are introduced for only one purpose: to show how theological views, in this case views about how God is related to morality, affect ethical decisions and the way they are made. By examining our views on many ethical issues, we can become clearer about how we really think of the relation of God and the world. That is central to every theology. If we acknowledge that we cannot turn over our moral decisions to experts, that we must take personal responsibility in this area of our lives, then, quite directly, we need to take responsibility for a wider range of our beliefs, and that means for our theology.

6. Real Beliefs and Avowed Beliefs: Homosexuality Continued

To take responsibility for our theology is not to invent it. All Christians already *are* theologians. We may not be much aware of what our beliefs are, and our beliefs may not be well thought through, but we do have life-shaping beliefs! To take responsibility for our theology is, first of all, to make explicit what we already believe.

This requires a further distinction. There are some doctrines that most of us suppose we *should* hold if we are to be Christian at all. There are other beliefs that actually shape our responses to what happens. These two sets of beliefs are rarely identical, although they usually overlap.

Both sets play a large role in relation to the positions of Christians on homosexuality. In this section and in section seven, we will examine how real beliefs are sometimes in tension with avowed beliefs. In this section we will pursue the issue of homosexuality through an imagined conversation between Henry Smith and his son, Bill, prompted by Bill's learning that one of his Christian friends is gay.

"Dad," asked Bill, "you have often spoken harshly, even contemptuously, about gays. Why do you reject their life-style so vehemently?"

"Son," replied Henry, "I guess it is first of all because I am a Bible-believing Christian, and the Bible condemns homosexuality severely."

"I suppose you're right, Dad, but frankly I don't remember hearing about that in church. Are homosexual acts a form of fornication?"

"They may be," answered Henry, "but the rejection is more explicit than that. In Leviticus it is said that a man who lies with another should be killed!"

"Do you believe that?" Bill wanted to know.

"Well, no, I suppose not," Henry acknowledged. "But it shows how strongly the Israelites felt about the matter."

"But, Dad, sometimes we are told that the Old Testament laws, such as those in Leviticus, don't apply to Christians. Do you agree with that?"

"That's a complicated business, son, especially because of Paul's

35

teaching about the law. So perhaps it is better to stick to Paul's own writings. Sometimes he lists homosexuality among the sins that Christians should stay away from. And in the first chapter of Romans he presents homosexuality as the extreme case of what happens when people turn away from God."

"That sounds like a pretty clear rejection, Dad, but when Tom told me that he had tried very hard to feel sexually attracted to girls, but just couldn't, it didn't sound to me as though he was turning away from God. It sounded to me like a cry for acceptance, even for forgiveness, from my most devoutly Christian friend. I just can't put him in that picture. Is it possible that Paul was wrong in thinking that turning away from God is the only thing that can lead to homosexual feelings and actions?"

"Maybe it isn't the only explanation for homosexuality," Henry admitted. "But the teaching of the Bible is so clear that I don't see how we can avoid condemning homosexuality. Maybe we shouldn't reject Tom for his feelings, but we should certainly insist that he not act on them."

"You mean that Tom should live his whole life without any sexual love at all? If I were Tom, I would find that awfully cruel teaching, wouldn't you?"

Henry was silent for a while. Finally he said, "The Christian faith demands a lot from us!"

But Bill was not satisfied. He knew that Tom was suffering terribly from his realization that he was different. Bill wanted something more positive to say to Tom than this. "Dad, I don't think this is fair. Maybe the explicit teachings in the Bible count against Tom's ever being sexually fulfilled. But there are other explicit teachings that you don't take that seriously. For example, Jesus opposed divorce, but I'm sure you support it sometimes. And Jesus had some very extreme things to say about owning property, but when I've been worried by them, you've assured me that his teachings don't apply literally to us. Why do you find a few passages against homosexuality so convincing when you find a way around the passages about money?"

Bill's question forced his father to ask himself a question he realized he had been avoiding. Was his strong feeling against homosexuality really based on the biblical passages he was citing?

Or had he turned to the Bible to find affirmation of feelings whose origins did not come primarily from there? "Son, you are probably right that I take the biblical condemnation of homosexuality more seriously than some other biblical teachings because I feel so deeply that homosexuality is wrong. It just isn't natural. The whole evolutionary process depends on the division of male and female. They exist for each other and for the propagation of their species. The Bible makes that very clear also in the story of creation. The biblical authors saw that homosexuality was unnatural, and so do I. It goes against the whole order of creation."

Bill was impressed by his dad's sincerity and by the power of his argument. If it were not for Tom, no doubt, he would just accept it and go on about his business. But what good would it do to tell Tom that his feelings for other fellows were "unnatural"? He had tried hard to have "natural" feelings for girls. "But, Dad, in Tom's case it seems that his attraction to other fellows is what *is* 'natural.' What does it really mean to say that it is 'unnatural' when it is the only kind of sexual feeling he has? Does that mean that *he* is unnatural? But why would God make someone 'unnatural'?"

"Son, you're pushing me farther than I really know how to go. I agree with you that Tom seems like a fine boy and a serious Christian. I am pained that he says he is gay. A lot of people who, like me, reject homosexuality seem to believe that homosexuals could just choose not to be that way. But what I have read about it indicates that is true only for some who are borderline, who have feelings both ways. There's a lot of debate about whether homosexuals are that way genetically or because of what happens in the first two years of life. But that doesn't seem to make a lot of difference. In either case, by the time they become aware of their sexual feelings, there is not much they can do about them. I'm sure that Tom would prefer to have normal feelings for girls, date, get married, and have children. Instead of feeling revolted by his attraction to other fellows, I know I should feel primarily sympathy. But I still don't see how it can be right for him to act on his feelings. From what I have read about the gay life-style, it sounds disgusting and completely immoral."

"Tom is bothered about that, too, Dad. He has read a bit about

the life of gays, and most of what he has read sounds like extreme
promiscuity. He says he doesn't want that. But he does want
someone to love and to be faithful to. And he knows that there are
homosexual couples like that. Why is that wrong?"

"Son, the whole point of sex and faithfulness to one partner is
for the sake of having a family. But two men can't have children.
It just doesn't fit God's plan." Henry knew the answer was a bit
flat, but it was the best he could do. He wished Bill would accept it
and stop pushing him so hard. But at another level, he was very
proud of his son. Bill was truly concerned about Tom, and what
could be more Christian than that? He knew that he had not
satisfied Bill, and deep down he hoped Bill would keep pushing.

Bill did. "In our sex education class at the church, it was
emphasized that having children was just one reason for sex and
family. Even if we found out that we could not have children for
some reason, or even if we decided not to, we were encouraged to
share our lives with a single partner. If that is the best strategy for
men and women together, why is it not the best strategy for two
men who love each other and are not able to love women?"

"Son," Henry answered, "you make a lot of sense. The truth is
that when I have thought of homosexuals I have not thought
much about lifelong partnerships. I'm not sure that the biblical
passages I cited had those in mind either. I'll have to admit that in
my guts I don't like the whole idea. It is not even going to be easy
for me to treat Tom in a natural way now that I know how he
feels. But I know that as a Christian I should be especially
accepting of him now in his suffering. And I know that I don't
really know why he should remain always celibate rather than
finding a partner. If it is only because of my feelings that I
recommend celibacy, then I need to reconsider my feelings. But
I'm not at all sure of that. It still seems to me that the church has to
stand for heterosexual marriage and against all the aberrations.
But maybe that's just prejudice—what they call 'homophobia'
these days."

"Thanks, Dad, for talking with me. Whatever the real Christian
position is on this, I'm sure that your openness with me is an
important expression of the Christian character I so deeply
respect in you."

7. **Real Beliefs and Avowed Beliefs: Other Examples**

Two brief examples will help to indicate the complexity of the relation between beliefs that Christians avow because they think they are Christian and the ones that constitute their real convictions. First, consider the case of Edith Gutowski, in chapter 1, who prays with such a sense of intimacy with God. Even in her case, there may be a tension between her real beliefs and those she would assert if asked.

Her prayer life implies that she believes herself to interact with God. But when asked, she may reply that she knows that God does not change in any way whatsoever—that is, God is immutable. Taking that in its strictest form would mean that God is not affected by her prayers. If she becomes aware of the conflict, she may modify her avowed belief, asserting that by "immutability" she means only that God is faithful and steadfast in love and mercy. This would bring her avowed belief in harmony with what comes to expression in her prayers. On the other hand, she might feel the pressure to change her way of praying to bring it more in line with what she understood to be the church's teaching.

Consider a quite different example. Lois McNutt is a Christian who has Jewish friends. In the church she hears that only those who confess Jesus as their Savior can be saved. She deeply believes that being saved is a very important matter. Yet, she never invites her Jewish friends to come with her to church or witnesses to them of her own faith. Indeed, she does not really feel that she should. Her feeling is that it would be the wrong thing to do.

If Lois is asked the question of whether people can be saved apart from Jesus, she will probably answer no. This is the belief she understands that she is supposed to hold. But the belief expressed in her real feelings and conscientious actions is something different. It is that the Jewish friends can be saved through their Jewish faith.

When she brings all of this to consciousness, she is confused. She sometimes accuses herself of being too weak and too cowardly to share the gospel with her friends. At other times she explains to herself that it is hopeless or useless. But deep down she does not really think of them as damned, and her actions give expression to her *real* beliefs.

Real beliefs and avowed beliefs affect one another. In this case, the avowal of the belief that the Jews cannot be saved unless they become Christians may eventually affect her deepest feeling about her friends. On the other hand, bringing to consciousness the *real* belief raises questions about whether she wants to continue avowing the one she understands that she should hold as a Christian.

8. Beginning Where You Are

No generalizations are possible about whether one set of beliefs is better or worse, more or less Christian, than another. Sometimes our deepest feelings are more Christian than what we are told Christians should believe. Sometimes these deepest feelings are wholly unconverted and need to be changed through internalization of the avowed beliefs.

At this stage in the argument, this is not the question. The plea is to bring your true beliefs into the light of day, to become aware of what you really believe. Only then can you take responsibility for your beliefs. In chapter 3 we will consider some ways of evaluating these beliefs.

Taking responsibility may have diverse consequences. At one extreme, you may simply confess what your real beliefs have been and repudiate them. It may take time to uproot them, but when you view them in the light of day, you may recognize that they cannot be justified. At the other extreme, these real beliefs may become a center around which you develop an authentic theological position. Or you may modify both the underlying beliefs and the ones that seem more explicitly Christian as their relation is clarified.

In this chapter, I have said nothing of whether one theology is better than another or of how this might be judged. This is a very important question, and indeed the rest of the book will be a response to it. But there is little point in discussing how your theology is to be evaluated and improved if you do not know what your theology is.

Too often people write as if we Christians were to begin with a

40

blank slate, look around at other people's theologies, and then apply a particular set of criteria in deciding among them. That process, artificial as it is, *might* lead to avowing commitment to one theological system or another. It is unlikely to make of that adopted theology our *real* theology. That kind of model is too often, if very vaguely, in people's minds, and it shares responsibility for the inauthenticity of so many statements about theology. Too many of us think that theology is the recitation of doctrines that we *should* accept. We can be excused for not wanting to devote a lot of time and serious thought to puzzling that out.

The burden of this chapter is to set aside that approach to theology. The only place that authentic theology can begin is with the real beliefs of real Christians. Much may be wrong with those, but that is not the question. We can grow theologically only if we discover for ourselves that our beliefs are not adequate or appropriate. To abandon real beliefs because someone else tells us they are not orthodox only encourages the inauthenticity of which I have repeatedly spoken.

You may change real beliefs on discovery of the reasons for the church's rejection of those beliefs in the past. That can be an authentic theological development. But, like all authentic theological development, it can begin only where you really are. The first step from where you already are is the recognition of where you are. That is what this chapter has been mainly about.

DOING YOUR THEOLOGY

1. State your position on abortion, capitalism, or homosexuality. Do you assert that position as a Christian? Explain.
2. Does your explanation fit with any of the ways of relating God and morality outlined in section four? If so, which one? If not, explain your view of the relation. Formulate your justification of your position in a way that shows its grounding in your view of the relation of God and morality.
3. Show how, with the same view of this relation, one could argue for a different moral judgment on the topic you have chosen. Determine what makes the difference and how the issue could be adjudicated.

41

4. Choose another moral issue and go through the same analysis. Possible topics: euthanasia, divorce, masturbation, participation in war, recreational hunting.
5. Recognizing that Christians relate God and morality in different ways, justify your belief. Do you follow it consistently? That is, do your arguments on all moral issues follow this pattern when it is relevant? Or do you appeal to the relation to God in different ways on different issues? If you are not consistent, can you justify your inconsistency? Or does your inconsistency suggest that your moral views have a different basis from the one you have articulated, and that your justifications are rationalizations—that is, arguments offered to support positions actually held for other reasons? If the latter, can you justify that?

CHAPTER THREE

Shaping Up

1. Preparing to Evaluate

*T*he first step in taking responsibility for our beliefs is to find out what they are. This is what the Reformers called for. The Roman Catholic Church had taught that people can be saved by an implicit faith. It sufficed that they were prepared to accept the authority of the Church, so that they would believe what they were told. To the eyes of the Reformers that appeared to replace faith in God with faith in the church. They taught that faith should be explicit. Only in that way could it be truly personal.

This is no longer a way of distinguishing Protestants and Catholics. Especially since Vatican II, Roman Catholics have been working harder and more successfully than Protestants to make beliefs explicit. Protestants have much to learn from them in this regard.

Unfortunately, explicit beliefs can be bad ones. They may be good, and for Christians they can't all be bad. But sincere Christians have done many terrible things just because of what they believe. For example, because they believed that Jews were damned for rejecting Jesus, many Christians have persecuted them, hoping to make them believe. Christians have waged war on "infidels," tortured those they suspected of heresy, and destroyed whole cultures because of sincerely held beliefs. Those whom we call saints were often leaders in these destructive actions. Making our real beliefs explicit is an indispensable start on the way to a good theology, but it is only that. The next task is to become more genuinely Christian in our beliefs.

Unfortunately, some Christians have thought the way to improve their theology is to submit themselves to external authority. The fear that this is expected or demanded often prevents honest discussion of theology. There are times and places where churches have demanded this. But this book emphatically does not support this theory. From my point of view, beliefs can be improved, made more Christian, only as real convictions are changed by new insights, convincing arguments, or deepening experience. This is a lifelong process, not something we achieve by turning our minds over to an institution or an expert to be reshaped.

The previous chapter showed that making implicit beliefs explicit affects them. Tension between beliefs evokes a natural human tendency to seek consistency. This tendency is rationality. The realization that we are being inconsistent makes us uncomfortable. Sometimes we decide to live with inconsistencies. But then we need to think up good reasons for doing so. For example, we may decide that God is so different from everything else we know that our ideas about God can never be consistent. We may then talk about mystery or paradox and do so with some contentment. But most of the time, for most purposes, most of us prefer not to contradict ourselves too blatantly.

One step beyond making beliefs explicit was already introduced in the previous chapter. Quite spontaneously, reason goes to work on conscious beliefs as it cannot on unconscious ones. This is a gain. Making beliefs conscious tends to move them toward consistency.

There can be no assurance that the press toward consistency will subordinate the less Christian belief to the more Christian one. Sometimes it gives priority to a belief that is *supposed* to be more Christian, but that is not truly so. If, for example, Lois McNutt, the woman with the Jewish friends, decided that she should accept the doctrine that no one is saved apart from faith in Christ, because she supposed it to be more Christian, her actual relations with her friends might, from many other points of view, become less Christian.

44

2. Identifying the Sources of Beliefs

This brings us to the next step. How can we decide which beliefs are more Christian, which less? This is a question of norms, authorities, or guidelines. It is itself a theological question. We cannot first formulate an answer independent of other beliefs, and then judge these other beliefs by this answer. Decisions about norms emerge in the process of reflecting about all the other beliefs.

For this reason, there was no clear separation in chapters 1 and 2 between the doctrines that people lived out of and their beliefs about norms. In the debate about using female images for God, for example, beliefs about how Scripture is authoritative were as directly involved as beliefs about God. No doubt, as the women had studied feminist literature, both their thinking about the Bible and their ideas of God had changed, and these changes had interacted with each other.

The next step, then, is not to turn away from our beliefs to discover some objective norms by which to check them. It is simply to examine the beliefs more closely, recognizing that these beliefs are about both doctrines and norms. Indeed, we can hardly maintain that distinction at all.

The best way to initiate this next step in our theological voyage is to ask where the beliefs came from. We can take up again the example of Henry Smith. He feels strongly that homosexuality is wrong. He argued first on the basis of particular scriptural texts, but when he saw that other texts, at least equally clear, did not convince him in the same way on issues of divorce and money, he realized that the real reason for his rejection was less the occasional texts than his revulsion against what he deeply felt to be unnatural. By the end of the conversation with his son, he was open to asking whether it is Christian to condemn all homosexual actions on the basis of his strong feelings that they are unnatural.

As a first step toward answering the question of where his beliefs came from, he can try to discover what caused him to feel that way. The most important issue to deal with first is whether his negative feeling arose naturally and rationally from the observation of the world. If so, there will be no need to modify his position. He will understand that he is seeing the patterns ordained by God in the natural world.

But it is more likely that self-examination will lead Smith to see that his strong feelings reflect the feelings and expressions of others, that they are culturally conditioned. He may decide that his feelings of revulsion about homosexuality result from the contemptuous tone of voice his father and friends used when referring to it. If so, he will not appeal to his own feelings of what is natural as a direct intuition of God's purposes.

He may turn to a closely related position that he finds to have been important in the tradition: natural law theory. Natural law theory does not appeal to feeling but to reason. According to natural law theory, whatever the psychological explanation of the depth of his feeling, the judgment connected with it and supportive of it is rational. Homosexuality is objectively unnatural.

According to this theory, we are all able to discern that the only natural role of sexuality is procreation. This can be justified in part by evolutionary theory. There can be little doubt that gender differentiation emerged as one of nature's successful strategies for reproduction. Its success, at least among human beings, among whom instinct is weaker, depended on the participants' enjoyment of the sexual act. In this sense, in "nature" procreation is primary, and enjoyment is secondary. Procreation was not usually the conscious purpose of those engaged in the sexual act. They more often sought enjoyment. But procreation was nature's, and therefore the Creator's, purpose in associating pleasure with sex.

This traditional argument from natural law can make sense in the context of modern knowledge, but it also has to be qualified more than conservative theorists are willing to do. The evolutionary process did not select for procreation alone. It selected also for stable social relations, and in the human case, that meant human bonding. The disconnection of sexual enjoyment from the menstrual cycle did not enhance reproduction, but it did enhance bonding. Hence we could say that the enjoyment of sexuality was in the service of mutual love. We might argue that sexual acts separated from love are not natural. Even this must be recognized as a quite special use of "natural," since it is obviously natural, in other, more usual, senses, to seek sexual pleasure as an end in itself.

The bonding facilitated by sexual enjoyment and contributory to social stability was primarily heterosexual. Consequently this long excursus on the justification of natural law theory does not directly challenge its point that the survival advantage of sexual enjoyment may have been only in its heterosexual form. Hence, as Smith reflects on natural law theory, he may not find his belief in the unnaturalness of homosexuality refuted. The best check on his real commitment to the argument is whether he is prepared to accept other conclusions drawn from it with equal consistency. The example of masturbation is a good test.

For a long time the church taught that masturbation is wrong because it is unnatural in the same sense as homosexuality. This was clearly true; there is no way that masturbation can produce children, nor does it contribute to the bonding that improves the survival capacity of the community. The argument against it, so far as natural law theory is concerned, is identical with that against homosexuality. If Smith's rejection of homosexuality is really based on this view of what is natural and unnatural, then he should judge masturbation in exactly the same light.

But let us suppose that Smith practiced masturbation as an adolescent with no ill effects. He felt no guilt about it then, and he feels none now. It seemed and seems quite natural to him. He does not propose to teach his own children that they must avoid it. From all he has read, he knows that such teaching does not stop masturbation; it only surrounds it with damaging guilt.

This exploration of the possibility of a rational basis for his direct judgment leads Smith in the end back to the recognition that his judgments have reflected his feelings. They did not arise from objective judgments of unnaturalness. His judgment for masturbation and against homosexuality resulted from the different judgments of these two phenomena in the community most influential on him. He accepts the fact that they are conditioned.

Still, the fact that he derived his feelings and judgments from others does not mean that what he feels is wrong. To argue in that way would disqualify everything in ourselves that expresses the influence of Christianity! Examination of most beliefs shows that

47

they are culturally conditioned. The question is rarely Are they conditioned? The questions are these: By what are they conditioned? Why have others originated and passed on to us these ideas or attitudes?

The issue, then, is why his father and his friends had these attitudes. Since they were not especially reflective about their feelings, that just pushes the question back a step: Where in general did this cultural attitude come from?

3. The Authority of the Bible

Smith might reasonably conclude that his strong feelings resulted from his immersion in the Christian tradition. If his concern is to determine how Christian his beliefs are, this is certainly not an argument against them! On the other hand, the dominance of a belief through most of the tradition does not guarantee that it is right. If the belief dominated the tradition chiefly because of its derivation from natural law theory, and if that theory does not seem to Smith a valid basis for a total condemnation of homosexuality, then the argument is not strong.

However, Smith could decide, instead, that the deepest reason for the tradition's opposition to homosexuality was its faithfulness to the Bible. For any Christian this must count in favor of continuing the tradition. But even if biblical opposition, faithfully transmitted through the tradition, is the deepest reason for the present feeling, the issue is not settled. The question of whether it is now Christian to continue the opposition remains.

The issue here is the Christian relation to the Bible. In his conversation with his son (see chapter 2, section six), Smith decided that despite his explicit appeal to biblical texts, it was not the absolute authority of the Bible on every topic that grounded his own strong opposition to homosexuality. He turned from biblicism to the judgment of unnaturalness to ground his opposition. Now he has come, through the analysis of the sources of his own feelings, back to the Bible. He must ask, Does the Bible have the kind of authority that can bring this quest to an end at this point? In other words, if the Bible is the source of the tradition in which he stands, a tradition that has been fairly consistent through Christian history, doesn't that suffice?

The answer for most of us, whether we explicitly avow it or not, is no. On *some* issues we do not feel bound to the explicit teachings of Bible and tradition even when they speak with some consistency. For example, in this century most Protestants have decided that divorce is the most Christian alternative under some circumstances, despite Jesus' condemnation and the consistent opposition of the dominant tradition down until that time. Does that mean there is another source of authority for us, or are we free to pick and choose what we like?

These formulations are misleading. Christians as Christians are not free to reject Scripture and tradition unless Scripture and tradition provide positive reasons for doing so. But most Christians believe that, indeed, on some points such reasons can be found.

The most obvious examples are from the relation of the Bible and tradition to the natural sciences. For many centuries some Christians tried to derive their science from the Bible. Others depended on the knowledge inherited from the Greeks. Few accented the tensions between these sources. But this barely noticed compromise could not be maintained in the face of modern astronomy and other sciences. For very few Christians today does the unanimity of Scripture and tradition on some point of astronomy commit them to the acceptance of that view. At least to some extent, in actual practice if not in avowed theory, Christians follow Roger Schwartz, the businessman of chapter 2, in limiting the authority of Scripture to certain fields and turning to modern authorities in others.

Is this move that virtually all Christians make simply an inescapable compromise between Scripture and tradition, on the one side, and the demands of modernity on the other? Some experience it as such. But within the tradition itself it has been worked through in a more positive light.

Students of the Bible have pointed out that the pre-scientific ideas that were obviously in the minds of the writers were never the topic under discussion or the point to be made. Acceptance of the writers' message does not require acceptance of their worldview. Modern people may have to reformulate the language, but they can express much the same point in language that makes sense. Accepting the *message* of the Bible and acknowledging its authority do not depend on astronomy or physics.

This distinction supports the separation of the moral and religious spheres, to which the Bible does speak, from the scientific ones, to which it does not. But this successful move within the tradition, based on study of the Bible, leaves many questions unsettled.

The most important issues center now on the social sciences. These were raised by the story of Schwartz, who was angry at the pastor's sermon criticizing the pursuit of gain (chapter 2, section 3). The attacks on the rich scattered through both Testaments are not mere background for some other message! Hence their importance to the biblical message cannot be minimized as can biblical comments on astronomy. On the contrary, the denunciation of the love of money is one of the most often repeated biblical points. It is far more central than any teaching about sexuality. If this critique of selfishness in the area of economics is surrendered, it must be on some other basis!

That basis was spelled out by Schwartz. Our modern scholars have learned things about the workings of society that the biblical writers did not know. These have quite different implications for the moral way of pursuing business than do the explicit biblical statements. These biblical statements were made in ignorance. Now that we know better, we cannot repeat them.

Whereas the study of the Bible's own intention warranted the acceptance of new knowledge about the natural world, the acceptance of Schwartz's theology seems to require a compromise between the authority of the Bible and tradition, on the one side, and of modern knowledge, on the other. Indeed, on a very important issue, it seems to require giving precedence to the latter.

In practice, for the most part, rightly or wrongly, the church has made that compromise and yielded to the authority of the social as well as the physical sciences. But the rationale has not been worked out well. Section two in chapter 4 will take up this urgent question again, and chapter 7 will discuss another aspect of the right relation of Christians to the authority of modern thought.

The question of homosexuality raises analogous, but different, issues about biblical authority. Unlike the pursuit of wealth, this topic is treated only tangentially in the Bible. For example, within lists of sins in the New Testament can be found Greek words that probably referred to, or included within their range, some specific types of homosexual practice. Even in the place where attention is most specifically drawn to homosexual practices (Rom. 1:26-27), the passage is not written for moral exhortation but to show the terrible consequences of human rebellion. Again, a specific homosexual practice is used as a climactic indication of the consequences of sin. There is no doubt that Paul is revolted by the practice in question. But there is a question of whether this necessarily implies rejection of loving homosexual activity within faithful relationships by those who are disinclined to heterosexual love. Indeed, it clearly does not have these in mind.

Since sexual teaching is incidental to the points being made, it could be treated in the same way as the Bible's pre-scientific cosmology. With each New Testament passage in which reference to some type of homosexual activity is made, we can ask, What is the point of this passage? This point can then be made with different examples or formulated in a way that makes clear that what are condemned primarily are certain perversions of sexuality, both heterosexual and homosexual.

But to say that this way of dealing with the biblical testimony is possible does not by itself recommend it. If the church is right to argue that homosexual acts are always wrong, then it is also right to accent the negative attitudes toward certain forms of homosexuality that some of its writers, especially Paul, express.

How do we Christians decide which way to go? At this point, most of us want factual information about homosexuality derived from the psychological and social sciences. When Paul is giving full expression to his horror and disgust, he speaks of men and women "giving up" natural heterosexual relations. This can, of course, happen. Men and women who are normally attracted chiefly to members of the opposite sex can "give up" those relations in order to explore homosexual ones.

Some believe that all homosexual actions are of this kind. They believe that homosexuals are responsible for choosing their orientation as well as for acting on it. Their model is really the bisexual who feels some attraction in both directions, and they judge it wrong for such persons to give up their capacities for heterosexual love and marriage in favor of homosexual relations.

This is not the place for discussing the appropriate ethics for the bisexual. The factual issue is whether this picture of homosexuality is correct. Clearly, it is not. There is still uncertainty as to whether homosexuality is genetically determined or formed by relations in infancy. But it is no longer possible to suppose that homosexual persons freely choose their sexual desires. As they enter adolescence, some children *find* themselves to be homosexuals. They do not choose this condition with all of the suffering it entails. They do not "give up" natural relations. For them, to engage in what heterosexuals regard as "natural" relations is very unnatural indeed.

If Smith has come this far in his reflections, he is near the end of his course. Precisely here he faces the question on which we Christians find it most difficult to come to a final decision. The issue is the authority of Scripture. We agree that it does have authority in the sphere of morality. We agree that that authority is not absolute. The broader call to love God and fellow creatures can lead to different moral judgments from those that appear incidentally, or even emphatically, in the Bible.

The reluctant acceptance of divorce by oldline denominations, out of compassion for the suffering that marriage sometimes engenders, is the clearest example of a major change of teaching. That is, the church uses the general moral principle to generate specifics that differ from the conclusions explicitly drawn in the Bible. The social context has changed sufficiently, the church believes, that the reasons for total prohibition of divorce no longer apply. This is a responsible Christian relation to scriptural authority.

Should this analogy be applied in the case of homosexuality? That is one possibility. But the analogy can be challenged. Divorce is reluctantly accepted as a necessary adjustment to the failure of an ideal. The proposal with respect to homosexuals is that the ideal of heterosexual marriage is not applicable. Much in the teaching of Jesus supports compassionate treatment of those who fail to meet ideal standards. Hence divorce can be justified. But it is harder to find a basis for changing the standards. Hence, it may be concluded, homosexual bonding cannot be supported.

Of course, the argument goes on. It can be replied that the truly basic standard is not heterosexual marriage. Actually, remarkably little is said about that. The truly basic standard is love. The church's love of homosexuals should encourage their faithful love of one another, not punish it.

Presumably, there is agreement that not everything in the Bible is to be given exactly the same weight. That means that some things can be set aside as unimportant for the biblical message, and others can be reinterpreted in the light of more basic teachings. How far does this go? And how do we Christians decide what is most basic?

4. Testing Beliefs

I have offered an example of the kind of reflection that tests and improves theology. It is only an example, but the example does show that the process of examining the sources of beliefs involves questions of many sorts, and that our answers to those questions move the reflection along. It also shows how wrestling with particular issues interacts with wrestling with questions of authority. Trying to work out the nature of the authority of Scripture and tradition apart from all particular questions of belief, and then applying the results, rarely works well. Each dispute raises the question of biblical authority in a different way. Indeed, the course of reflection on a single topic brought up these questions in different ways at different times. Nevertheless, some generalization of the type of approach here recommended is now in order.

First, we Christians can only begin where we are in order to become what we are: theologians. Second, we bring our real beliefs to awareness and see how these relate to one another. Third, we undertake to justify these beliefs as Christians. Fourth, we check to see whether the reasons given in the justification are the real reasons for our judgments. In this process, we test the principles we propose against our willingness to stick with them consistently.

These four steps were taken in chapters 1 and 2. They lead to the clarification of some beliefs that Christians sincerely and consistently hold. They do not ensure that these are truly Christian beliefs. How can this be tested?

The first step in this next level of testing, the fifth in our sequence, is to ask, as reflectively as possible, what the actual sources are of either the judgments or the assumptions that genuinely underlie them. Realistically and honestly, the answer will usually be that these beliefs are derived from some segment of the community: parents, school, church, newspapers, or friends.

For example, Roger Schwartz, who believed that in the economic world each person should strive for as much profit as possible, learned that idea from his study of economics and from others who had studied it. The source is clear. He got his beliefs about the church's authority to teach in areas of morality and religion more diffusely perhaps. But directly and indirectly, they came from the church. The way he has put them together may have been derived from friends, or it may be an original creative idea of his own. Thus far the analysis is not so difficult.

The sixth step is to ask whether the source is Christian. In this instance, what is derived from the church passes muster. So the issue focuses on the economics. Does modern economics have Christian sources? Obviously it arose in a Christian, specifically Calvinist, country—Scotland—and its understanding of human nature reflects the suspicions of human goodness that are nourished by the strong emphasis on original sin.

The fact that an idea comes from Christian sources counts in its favor, but it does not guarantee that it is truly Christian. Similarly, the fact that an idea comes from outside Christianity gives it somewhat less authority for us, but it may still be an idea that we Christians should accept. Hence, the next question, the seventh step, is more critical and more difficult. Are the ideas themselves Christian? That means, are they ideas that we *should* hold today?

We may be obligated to accept modern economic theory and its ethical implications even if we can trace no influence of Christianity on economics at all. If it is a demonstrated body of truth, then there is an excellent Christian reason to accept it—namely, the Christian commitment to truth. And if its teaching about economic morality follows inescapably from true theory, then we must accept it, too. If it contradicts biblical teaching, then we must abandon the latter on this point.

There are no rules as to how to proceed to answer this final question of what is Christian. In the earlier steps some of the testing was fairly objective. Much of the example about Henry Smith, worked through in some detail above, illustrated these tests.

When a proposal is made, such as that based on natural law theory, you need to clarify the theory to make sure that it does in fact support the position being considered. If it does, then the second test is whether this is really the norm to which you are committed. This test requires the determination of what other consequences follow from the norm proposed. If you find that some of these consequences differ from the opinions you have held, then comes the tough decision. Once you have seen that the position you think you hold has implications you have not previously drawn, do you draw those implications? In other words, are you *really* convinced by your own argument, or does it turn out to be a rationalization of a conclusion you actually reached on other grounds?

In Smith's case, rationalization turned out to be a major factor. Hence, he had to go back to the drawing board, seeking to understand whether there was some other justification for maintaining the position that initially commended itself to him so strongly. He then sought the real source of his strong feelings against homosexuality. He found that they came to him from tradition mediated especially by the attitudes of his father and friends. This tradition was partly shaped by the natural law theory he rejected, but it also seemed to him to be rooted in Scripture. Hence the source was Christian. But was the judgment itself Christian? This is the ultimate question, one to which as yet Henry Smith has not found a confident answer.

The seventh step, the answering of that question, is all-inclusive, but an aspect of it can be lifted up as being of special importance and requiring special attention. For convenience, I will call it the eighth step. The other steps will inevitably lead back to Scripture. Even if Smith had finally claimed that his basic conviction was the truth of natural law theory, he would still have needed to ask whether the adoption of the authority of natural law is Christian, and that would have meant biblically justified. Finally, some biblical justification is always needed.

DOING YOUR THEOLOGY

1. Go back to the judgments you articulated in your responses to the questions at the end of chapter 2. Select one that you feel strongly about. Review how you justified it. Are you satisfied with that justification? Explain.
2. Examine your way of justifying your position in relation to the steps listed in section four of this chapter. Answers to questions at the end of chapter 2 dealt with the first four steps. It is now time to press the justification harder and further. Taking either a moral judgment or an assumption crucial to your justification as your starting point, ask the following questions:
   a. Where did you derive this belief?
   b. Is the source Christian?
   c. How is the source related to the Bible?
   d. Is the way you appeal to biblical authority here a way you would employ whenever it is applicable or only selectively?
   e. If you apply it selectively, can you justify this?
   f. If not, can you reformulate your view of biblical authority so that you can use it consistently?

CHAPTER FOUR

Biblical Authority

1. Introduction

*C*hapter 3 emphasized the authority of the Bible. On this
general question there is little dispute among Christians.
But what has already been said makes it clear that this is
not a simple matter. We cannot go to the Bible to learn
straightforwardly what kind of authority it has for us. We cannot
appeal to the authority of the Bible to inform us just what that
authority is. Biblical authority does not displace other forms of
authority. Yet in every example the question of whether a
position is Christian is the question of whether it can be justified
as biblical.

For example, if Schwartz holds that acceptance of the
normativeness of economic morality is the right position for the
Christian, finally he must show how the Bible indirectly justifies
it. If someone else argues that some forms of homosexual activity
are to be affirmed, then that person must provide a biblical basis
for that. The feminists in chapter 1 needed to show that some
reading of the Bible justifies a prophetic critique of biblical
language and imagery and even of the teachings of the prophets
themselves. However circuitous the route, theological thinking
cannot escape the question of *how* the Bible is authoritative. But it
is equally true that we cannot answer that question without
wrestling with concrete issues and testing what we say at every
stage in relation to what we *really* believe.

A very important part of this issue in most instances will be the relation of the Bible to extra-biblical materials. Almost everyone acknowledges that the Bible at least allows the use of other sources. Does it do more than that? Does it require that truth be accepted wherever it is found? Does it allow itself only to be supplemented by these other sources, or can it also be corrected and even replaced by them? Does this apply to all topics or only to some? If there are limits to the role of extra-biblical authorities, how are they determined? If there are no limits, what does it mean to speak of scriptural authority at all?

2. Biblical and Secular Authority

To abandon scriptural authority is to abandon Christian identity or, at least, an inclusive Christian identity. The case of Roger Schwartz can clarify this point. His position can be interpreted in two ways.

One possibility is that Schwartz believes that it is as a Christian that he accepts the truth of economics and its ethics, even when it contradicts important Christian ethical teaching. To believe that, he must believe that something about the biblical teaching points to the need of accepting scientific knowledge and drawing consistent conclusions from it. In this way he can maintain a unified Christian identity, using the Bible directly for some purposes and indirectly elsewhere, when he provides biblical justification for drawing from quite autonomous sources.

But his position may be different. It may be that whatever the Bible asserts, he, as a modern man, must and will correct and replace biblical teaching on the subject of economics. He may regard his position as a synthesis of the Christian and the economic one, rather than as a Christian one that has been transformed by economic knowledge. In this case, he has given up a unifying Christian identity and ceases to take part in the theological task. His identity is that of a modern man who draws on Christianity for some purposes. These purposes are determined from a position outside Christianity.

It is much healthier for the church and for us, its members, if we refuse to treat our beliefs as compromises between Christianity and something else, as in this second approach. It is better if we understand the incorporation of other beliefs, even those in

58

opposition to aspects of biblical teaching, as itself a Christian act. Hence, given these two choices, the church should support the former.

This point is especially important. One of the great weaknesses of the mainline Christian churches today is that most of their members do not take their Christian identity as all-important or all-embracing. Our businessman may consider himself both a Christian and a committed member of the business community, and he may put these two ways of identifying himself on the same level. He will then understand his beliefs as a compromise between his two loyalties. Or he may think of his position as a personal synthesis that is not directly an expression of either identity. In either case, Christian identity loses its primacy.

Many people have split their identity in some such way. Some split it between their church and their nation. Others think of themselves as members of the intelligentsia who can identify some parts of their lives and beliefs with the Christian church. Others think of themselves as both feminists and Christians.

People who have divided loyalties along these lines cannot really be Christian theologians in the sense for which this book calls. To be theologians is to desire that all the beliefs by which we live be Christian. It is to be dissatisfied with any beliefs that we cannot justify as Christian, even if we cannot readily give these up. For example, if we are not bothered by realizing that we place our country on an equal plane with God, then our identity is not decisively Christian. We may still hold some Christian ideas; we may support the church, but we will not engage in the struggle to shape theology.

One of the main reasons for the decline of theology is that so many Christians suppose that some of their most important beliefs are not Christian. To be Christian, they think, their beliefs must have a clear origin in the Bible or tradition. Yet they cannot live without beliefs that come from quite different sources. As a result, they understand their theology to include only one part of their real, life-determining belief system.

For example, many people derive much of their self-understanding from depth-psychological literature or from their own psychotherapeutic experience. This constitutes much of their real belief—that is, the belief that shapes their understanding and

59

evaluation of what is going on. Until they understand that theology has the task of integrating these other beliefs into a whole informed by the tradition, it will seem a minor and peripheral activity. As a result, their self-identification as Christians will also be subordinate. Churches made up of people like this can only be lukewarm.

For Christian identity to be fundamental and inclusive, we must find reasons within it for including much that comes from other sources. We must find those reasons within the Bible and the tradition. Hence, a central part of the theological task for each of us is to discern the ways in which the Bible and the tradition point beyond themselves to a larger truth.

3. Biblical and Historical Models

To find ways of incorporating new knowledge and under-standing into Christian faith, we can examine what happened through the history reflected in the Bible itself. Israel repeatedly assimilated the wisdom of other peoples, integrating into Judaism elements of the beliefs of the Canaanites, the Egyptians, the Babylonians, the Persians, the Greeks, and the Romans. Yet Israel was no less Jewish after a thousand years of assimilating wisdom from others than it was before.

Similarly Christianity, deriving from this Judaism, opened itself even more fully to the wisdom of the Greeks. When modern science arose, despite some tensions, Christianity integrated that into its vision, too. The modern historical consciousness and modern psychology have deeply affected it. Many of Christian-ity's most sensitive spiritual leaders are now incorporating elements of Eastern spirituality into their identity as well.

As long as Christian identity is intact, this incorporation is healthy and does not threaten the vitality of the church. Indeed, it expresses that vitality. It is only when there is a failure of nerve that the inevitable learning from others ceases to involve an integration into Christianity. Either there is no integration, or there is an integration of Christianity into something else. I have written this book in the hope of renewing a unifying Christian vision that can function as the real basis of life in the world.

Of course, the integration of alien elements into Christianity is always dangerous and sometimes pernicious. That is why it should be done reflectively. The incorporation of the best of Greek thought *was* done reflectively in the early church and in the Middle Ages. It made possible the triumph of Christianity in the classical world. But it also gave undue authority to some elements of the Greek tradition.

In later contexts, some elements of Greek thought that were assimilated into the tradition became an obstacle to fully authentic Christianity. We should learn from this history that all of our integrations are tentative and relative, the best we can do at the time. Therefore, the resulting form of the tradition is not an absolute authority.

I have illustrated this in relation to natural law theory. This theory is still quite influential today. It has been a valuable force in the modern world as an alternative to positivism. But it has wrongly claimed to be *the* Christian way of thinking, and it has led to policies that many find wrong, especially in the area of sexuality. It was *not* wrong to develop natural law theory in the integration of biblical and Greek thought in the Middle Ages. It *is* wrong to appeal to it as a final authority today.

4. The Wesleyan Quadrilateral

Sometimes, especially in the Wesleyan tradition, scholars speak of four authorities and call these "the quadrilateral." There is always the possibility that this talk of authorities can be authoritarian, as if theologians should submit their ideas successively to four external judges. But that is to misunderstand how these authorities really operate.

The point is, instead, that authentic theological work always deals with Scripture, with tradition, with experience, and with reason. All four are, for us Christians, internal—not external or imposed—norms. We cannot define them first, and then impose them on a theology from outside. What Scripture is as authority and how it functions as authority only emerge in the actual course of theological work. This is true of all the others. For this reason, I did not begin this chapter by listing these four authorities. But as we review what we have done, we can ask just how these four

61

norms have played a role, what role they have played, and whether reflecting about them can improve the theological work.

The four authorities are usually listed as above, giving pride of place, quite appropriately, to Scripture. For certain purposes this is fine. But if the purpose is to give realistic guidance to theological thinking, then it makes little sense to place one authority above the others as if it might overrule them. Each is, in its own way, decisive.

Some of us might think that the primacy of Scripture entails that we should always begin with Scripture. What could that mean? Perhaps we could pick up the Bible, open it at random, and ask what it says. But we do not derive from the Bible the choice of the Bible as the book to open. We make this choice because of immersion in a tradition that encourages it. Further, the Bible can say nothing until we ask questions, and the questions come out of each reader's historical situation, personal experience, and critical reflection.

In the discussions above, the effort to determine whether a belief is Christian always ended up by our questioning its relation to Scripture. This is what the primacy of Scripture really means. Directly or indirectly, each Christian affirmation must be justified by the character of the originating events of our faith. Often this relation is established through an indirect and critical approach. But if we are thinking as Christians, we cannot avoid this final test of what we affirm.

The following four sections will discuss the four authorities. What is said about them expresses what has been done in the preceding chapter. It is a more generalized or abstract statement of the ways in which Christian norms can test and improve conscious beliefs.

5. Experience

We will begin with experience. The experience in question is not identical with what Wesley had in mind; yet it is related to his intentions. This experience is your Christian experience, taken as broadly as possible, but focusing on those places where fundamental beliefs come most clearly to expression.

In one sense, this experience is a datum, rather than an

authority. But in the method proposed here, it is also an authority. At every stage you return to this question: What do I really believe? This is distinguished from what you may think the church expects in terms of your belief. If Scripture and tradition, used in a particular way, do not convince, then in the name of experience that appeal to their authority is rejected. What you *really* believe is the first and the last word. All the other norms enter in to render what you believe better, more Christian. Thus the goal is to *change* what you believe. In that sense, experience is anything but a final authority. But success in changing it is the only authority the others really possess.

Experience plays other roles as well. Although you begin and end in your personal experience, you should take very seriously the experience of others—all others. You are especially interested in the experience of other Christians. But you are also interested in religious experience as it takes form in other traditions. The time to segregate Christianity from the rest of the history of religion is past. The time to learn from others has come. Experience nurtured in radically different traditions is a peculiarly fruitful source of new insight.

Equally important is the experience of the oppressed. Through the centuries, North Atlantic white male theologians had not realized that they gave voice only to the experience of the privileged, indeed, of the oppressor. Once liberation theologians, beginning with African-American theologians, demonstrated that fact, theology, in principle, took on a new form.

We who are white and male still begin in our white male experience. We have no other place to start. But now we know that this experience is white and male, and very slowly we are learning to take account of that limitation as we think about the beliefs we hold. When we recognize that we feel and think as we do because we are white and male, and especially if we see that patterns derived from these feelings and thoughts are oppressive of others, we acknowledge that these are not Christian, even if they derive from the tradition. After all, the dominant tradition has been white and male for a long time.

Those who are not white and male have been particularly liberated to examine their experience as it really is, instead of the way white males have described it. Their eyes have been opened to much in personal relations and in society that had not been noticed before. Very much in the tradition, and even in the Bible, loses its authority when its origin in patriarchy becomes manifest. The sheer diversity of experience in itself warns against the theological generalizations of the past that described the human need of all to be identical. Becoming a theologian today is a quite different opportunity and challenge than it has ever been in the past.

6. Reason

Reason comes next, or is already involved with experience from the beginning. The effort to determine what you *really* believe—that is, the beliefs that shape your life—involves reason. As these beliefs emerge into consciousness, the way they relate to one another involves reason. Questioning their sources is a rational activity, as is every stage in the process of answering. This reason cannot be subordinated to anything else. Reason is involved in attributing authority to tradition and Scripture and determining just how they function as authorities. Reason has played an enormous role in the development of the content of Scripture and tradition, and it still plays that role in the further advance of tradition. Every interpretation of Scripture and tradition is an act of reason. It makes no sense to rank any other authority above reason.

Reason can also be taken to refer to a body of material—such as Greek philosophy, modern science, or contemporary psychology—that does not appeal to the authority of Christian tradition or Scripture. That is quite appropriate.

Of course, these bodies of thought do not reflect pure reason. They, too, depend on particular forms of experience and tradition, and modern science and contemporary psychology are more influenced than they usually acknowledge by the Christian Scripture. There is no reason that is not affected by experience and tradition. Reason in this sense has authority, but it needs to be integrated, by reason, of course, into a whole whose center is in Scripture.

Reason does not simply leave things as they are. It is the element of creativity or originality in thought. When you look for some way to integrate two ideas or insights, the hope is that reason will operate. Otherwise nothing new emerges; the two ideas just lie there inert, probably inconsistent, side by side. The vitality of Judaism and Christianity through the centuries is to be found in reason.

The hesitation to give so large a role to reason stems from the notion that it is more fully embodied in philosophy and science than in theology. That is true when theology is an authoritarian imposition of unauthentic beliefs. But that is not the theology I propose in this book. This theology is the embodiment of reason through and through. Indeed, this embodiment is even purer than that in most philosophy and science today.

The authority of reason in the quadrilateral is not primarily the testing of what you have done by logical principles or by comparison with some scheme of thought developed independently of Christian faith. It is your creativity coming to deeper understanding, more clarity, and greater comprehensiveness. If you find help in some philosophy, that is fine. And you will certainly want to test your views against whatever evidence you can find anywhere. But the greatest need is to *think*.

7. Tradition

The adjective *traditional* has come to mean little more than "conventional" or even "habitual." This is not entirely misleading. The traditions that have shaped us certainly do establish conventions and habits. But when we speak of tradition as a norm for theology, we do not mean whatever happens to be common practice in a particular community. We refer instead to a history of reflective thought and practice that has creatively shaped our culture. The Christian tradition has consciously identified normative elements within itself and uses these to criticize unreflective conventions and habits, even those found in the churches. Appealing to tradition is not always in support of continuing in comfortable, accustomed paths.

The source from which we derive beliefs in general is tradition. This tradition is not limited to the Christian tradition, narrowly conceived or even broadly conceived. It is the whole of the culture. Culture is the transmission of traditions of one sort or another. For those of us in Christendom, the sorting out of the specific contributions of the Christian tradition within the whole of the culture is very difficult indeed. Sometimes it is important, sometimes not.

Our experience and reasoning do not merely *arise* out of tradition; they are part of it. This is as true when they involve novel ideas and criticisms of past forms of the tradition as when they pass it on intact. Indeed, when they pass it on verbally unchanged, they may be turning it into something lifeless. We participate most fully in the Christian tradition when we are most alive, and that means when we are most original and creative. In this sense the tradition is no more an external authority than are experience and reason.

But just as reason can name a body of thought that exists quite objectively to us and must be dealt with, so can tradition. Tradition can mean what major Christian thinkers have taught in the past. They would not be major thinkers if their own work had not participated in tradition in a living way. But there is always the danger that it has become a congealed body of ideas to which some later theologians believe they should subordinate their own creative insights and honest convictions. In this sense, tradition can become a threat to authentic theology.

But the danger that the work of past thinkers can be used oppressively, and in authoritarian ways, should not prevent present thinkers from attributing to those past thinkers a very real authority. They formulated some ideas in ways that have commended themselves to the experience and reason of many Christians. These formulations may commend themselves to us as well. Even if they do not immediately commend themselves, that is not sufficient reason for us to dismiss them. Perhaps we have not yet asked the question to which these ideas are the answer. Unless we are personally convinced, we cannot reassert what they have said. But even if the only authentic response now possible is explicit rejection, we should remain provisionally open to the possibility that, at some later time, we can appropriate more from those thinkers. This is what it means to treat a past thinker as an authority.

The realization that all that we are and think is formed in tradition also gives it authority. We owe to it what we are, for good and ill. Even the principles by which we criticize it arise from it. We are in tradition as a fish is in water, only more fully, since tradition is in us too. Thus there is no question of the importance of tradition.

The only issue is the special importance of the Christian part of the whole tradition. The tradition that shapes us as American Christians contains within itself elements that may not be distinctively Christian. The Christian part of the whole tradition that shapes us requires of us that, as we become better theologians, we make distinctions and sort out what is Christian in the tradition.

This means that my language has been slightly misleading. We are not mere products of the past. We also respond to the past, and there is an element of freedom in that response. That is where reason comes into play—in the decision of response. We could have made other decisions resulting in selecting from the whole tradition in other ways. This might result in becoming primarily Americans, for example, who are only secondarily concerned with our inheritance from Christianity. We are not now compelled by the whole tradition in which we participate to continue a Christian identity. It is the selection of the Christian element within the total, partly Christian, American tradition as decisive that gives us Christian identity.

Hence, although most American Christians are Christians because our tradition made us so, we are not Christians without consenting to be Christians. For some of us, that has been a very conscious decision. For others, it has not. That decision, once made, is part of the ongoing tradition. But the decision is free, and so are the many other decisions we make at every turn as we engage in theology. We make none of them without the tradition, but exactly what features of the tradition we employ and exactly how we use them are acts of reason, and therefore of freedom.

The Christian tradition gives Christian identity, and the choice of Christian identity gives authority to the Christian tradition. We would not choose it if we did not find it convincing. But we would not find it convincing as a whole except as it already informs us. It is and remains convincing only as we work with it selectively and creatively. It becomes for us liberating and empowering, but only because, for us, it does not have a purely objective authority.

Viewed from without, as an inert body of congealed conclusions, it is full of muddleheadedness, error, and danger. Viewed from within, by participants, it is the basis of creativity, self-criticism, and wisdom.

8. Scripture

The Bible is part of the tradition. On this point, Catholics have spoken more wisely than have Protestants. The Bible comes to each generation through the whole tradition. The effort to jump over the later tradition to allow the Bible to speak directly is doomed to self-deception. The effort itself arises out of particular aspects of the tradition and cannot be separated from other parts of it.

But the Bible does have unique authority. That conviction comes through the remainder of the tradition much more than from the Bible itself. The remainder of the tradition has judged itself in the light of the Bible. Sometimes this judgment has been severely critical and has led to radical reformations. To choose Christian identity is to choose to share in a tradition that judges itself repeatedly in relation to the Bible.

But the appeal to biblical authority characteristic of the tradition has many forms. There is a tradition of discussion of this authority. That tradition has an authority that is not merely derived from the Bible it discusses. We cannot separate the authority of the Bible from the authority of the tradition that assigns it authority and determines just what that authority may be and how it functions.

Furthermore, the Bible itself embodies a long tradition. It is a creative tradition of repeated self-transformation. The Bible can only have the sort of authority that a tradition can have. This is very different from the sort of authority than may, wrongly in my view, be claimed for a creed. A creed can *claim* to be the congealed expression of the truth cumulatively developed through complex historical processes, rather than just one step in the whole movement of tradition. Fortunately, since there is no creedal summary in the Bible, there is no danger of this distortion. The Bible is a rich story of complex movements and the emergence of extraordinary individuals with revolutionary ways of seeing the world and of acting.

The authority of the Bible is, above all, that it is the formative story for all Christians. That history has entered into our being and made us what we are. It is a story of sin and righteousness, of defeat and victory. When they are not turned into moral homilies, the stories are inexhaustibly rich and throw light on every aspect of life. When the Bible is not turned into proof texts intended to put an end to free and creative thinking, it can inform theology with continually new challenges and suggestions. If theological work does not flow forth from the Scriptures, continuing the tradition whose origins are there, then it fails in a crucial test. To continue that tradition is to continue its adventure, its spirit, its courage, and above all its faith, hope, and love. To do that is not to repeat its words or even its specific beliefs. It is to be moved by the same Spirit that moved in those days and that continues to lead into new truth.

We Christians call the Bible "the Word of God." That has nothing to do with verbal dictation or the divine guarantee of inerrancy. Further, we can meet God in our own experience and in the whole of the tradition as well as in the Bible. In our freedom to think, which is called reason, God is peculiarly present. But we find that all of this finally depends on the Bible. Our knowledge of God is formed in and through the Bible. However critical we may be of particular biblical teachings, it is by what we have come to believe about the God who speaks to us in and through the Bible that we judge those teachings. The Bible is the Word of God for us, and we believe that it can become the Word of God for others, too.

9. Jesus Christ

The list of four norms or authorities omits the one that has been for most Christians decisive: Jesus Christ. Of course, those who use the "quadrilateral" insist that this norm is included in, even central to, Scripture. That is true, but it is true in much the same way that Scripture is included in tradition. Identifying as authoritative the tradition that includes Scripture does not justify the omission of Scripture as an authority. In the same way, the affirmation of Scripture as authoritative should not cause us to fail to make explicit the authority of Jesus Christ. The whole tradition testifies to the Bible as its norm. The whole of the Bible, read through Christian eyes, testifies to Christ.

In the examples given to show how theological reasoning can develop, raising new issues all along the way, I said very little about Christ. There was a reason. I tried at every point to leave the final judgment open. I wanted to show how the reasoning could proceed, how old arguments could give way, and how the issue could be newly posed. I did not want to present the arguments as leading only to my own conclusions.

I did speak of having to select a center within the Bible in the light of which other biblical ideas and teachings would be viewed. For me, as for most Christians, that center is Jesus Christ. Once I have said that, for me the issue with which Henry Smith wrestled is settled. The question has been whether Christians should condemn homosexuals for any overt expression of their feelings. That would include sexual relations in the context of mutual faithfulness and mutual love. In the name of Jesus Christ, I cannot condemn that. And for me, that is decisive.

There are other ways of appealing to Christ with opposite results, and I could have left the issue open even here. But that would be, for me, an uncomfortable game, one I choose not to play. Denying fellow human beings the joys of intimacy and physical love that I claim for myself would be cruel. I cannot connect that cruelty with Jesus Christ.

That does not mean that all homosexuals, or all heterosexuals, should seek sexual partners. Some are called to celibacy. But to assume, quite against the evidence, that all homosexuals are called to such celibacy, and to force them to choose between celibacy and the moral condemnation of the church, is, indeed, cruel. People are not made for the law; the law is made for them.

I have concluded this chapter confessionally, rather than descriptively. Theology is finally a confessional activity. That is why it begins with an individual's Christian experience. It ends there also. My Christian experience makes certain beliefs impossible for me. I try to remain open to the differing views of others, both to their confession of their experience and to their arguments. I do not want to condemn them for different

70

conclusions. But in the end, I cannot go beyond the experience of Jesus Christ that has been formed and reformed in more than forty years of theological reflection. Perhaps tomorrow more light will come, but I must speak from the experience I have today.

DOING YOUR THEOLOGY

1. How do you relate biblical authority to extra-biblical authorities? Show how this has operated in your justifications of your judgments in answering question 2 at the end of chapter 3.
2. How do experience, reason, and tradition operate in your Christian reasoning in relation to Scripture? Explain the similarities and differences with the proposal made in this chapter. Show how your view of these relationships has operated in your earlier arguments.
3. If your reflection on these matters has altered your initial judgments or the ways you justify them, state your present views on one of the positions you discussed in your previous writing and explain how and why it is different.

71

CHAPTER FIVE

Christians and Jews

1. Introduction

*I*n chapter 2 we met, very briefly, Lois McNutt. She was deeply concerned about a very important question: whether Christians are called to try to convert Jews. Since then we have considered other topics more rigorously and dealt with issues of methodology and authority. It is time to return to this topic through conversations between Ms. McNutt and several seminary professors.

This discussion will serve two purposes. First, it is another, more detailed, example of theological reflection that can stimulate your own. Second, it will suggest what professional theologians can and cannot contribute to you as you become a better theologian. Chapter 6 discusses this second topic directly.

Lois McNutt is a widow, fifty years of age, who has worked devotedly in the church for many years. She has been active in study groups sponsored by the women's organization. She has read more books on religion than have most laypeople, and she knows something about what is going on in the church beyond the local level. She was left financially secure by her husband; so she is able to give her time to volunteer work in the church and the community. She met her Jewish friends through her community work. These friends are very important to her. She is puzzled as to how to evaluate their faith, and she has the time, the energy, and the experience to investigate further.

The question that has become important to her is how to

reconcile her understanding of what the church teaches about salvation through Jesus Christ and her own deep feeling that her Jewish friends gain, through their faith, much of what she has gained through hers. She does not doubt the importance of Jesus Christ. Her own faith is bound up with him, but does that entail the exclusive statements about salvation that she has read in her Bible, finds in her liturgy, and sometimes hears from the pulpit?

The theological school in her city happens not to be an affiliate of her own denomination, but she has heard a couple of the professors speak. She has even been to the school twice to hear well-known visiting scholars. So she decides that instead of talking with her lay friends or with her pastor, she will make contact with one of the professors.

Whom on the faculty should she contact? She goes to the school and picks up a catalog. There are no courses on Christian-Jewish relations, but there is a professor of missions and evangelism. She sees that her question is very much related to that. Are Jews among the people Christians should try to convert? The same professor, Dr. Lesley Schmidt, also teaches courses on "ecumenics." That seems to approach matters from the other side. Lois knows that there is a National Conference of Christians and Jews, and that seems to be an approach that includes Jews with Christians in much the way the local council of churches includes a lot of Protestant denominations. Surely the professor can tell her what is the right way for Christians to relate to Jews and why.

2. Professor Schmidt—Ecumenism and Missions

Lois calls up Dr. Schmidt, explains her concerns very briefly, and asks for an appointment to speak with the professor. Dr. Schmidt is pleased to give her one. It is rare indeed that a layperson asks for his help. They agree to meet on the following Tuesday afternoon.

After Ms. McNutt and Dr. Schmidt have shaken hands and seated themselves, she explains her concerns in somewhat more detail and asks Schmidt for his opinion. Professor Schmidt replies as follows.

"There is no doubt that the starting point for Christian relations to non-Christians has been the proclamation of Jesus

73

Christ. New Testament teachings call for that very clearly, none more clearly than the concluding verses of Matthew: 'Go therefore and make disciples of all nations, baptizing them in the name of the Father and of the Son and of the Holy Spirit, and teaching them to obey everything that I have commanded you. And remember, I am with you always, to the end of the age' [Matt. 28:19-20]. I take the Great Commission as my point of departure as a former overseas missionary and one committed to the global mission. It does not seem to make room for any exceptions.

"But over the years Christians have learned that there are times and places for everything. We need to be 'wise as serpents' as well as 'harmless as doves.' Some kinds of missions at some times and places seems to do more harm than good. Direct evangelistic missions among Muslims, for example, have had almost no success and have created ill will. It seems better in Muslim countries to offer help in education or social work than to try to obey the Great Commission directly. Maybe someday it will turn out that Christian service was a way of discipling Muslims.

"I know you want to talk about Jews rather than Muslims. As I teach missions today, I emphasize that we cannot treat everyone who is not a Christian in the same way. I just now used the Muslims as an example. We have to decide what the Christian mission is in each case. Sometimes it is direct evangelism; sometimes it is giving a cup of cold water in the name of Jesus. In the case of the Jews today, it seems to be the most difficult task of all—leaving them alone!

"Of course, that's an exaggeration. They don't want pressure from us to convert. And they don't want charity. Above all, they don't want our meddling. But they do want us to understand them, and sometimes they want our support."

Ms. McNutt is delighted by what she hears, but she is not at all sure that it really answers her question. "In talking about the Jews, Dr. Schmidt, you have put all the emphasis on what *they* want. The Great Commission doesn't talk about asking people what they want and then providing it. Hitler wanted to rule the world, but no one thought that it was the Christian's task to accommodate him. I know that isn't what you mean, but I do need more help."

"Of course, you are right," Schmidt answers. "I was assuming a lot that I didn't express. We don't just try to please other communities. We have our own agenda. Yet, the only time when missions could ignore the question of what people wanted was when they were closely bound up with wars of conquest and with colonial rule. In that context, there were extreme cases in which people could be converted whether they liked it or not. Or they could be made to want conversion by being confronted with awful alternatives. None of us today take that as a good model.

"We want people to want to be Christian. So we try to present Christianity in a way that attracts people. We want them to hear the gospel as good news. When we find that the words we speak don't sound attractive to others, we may try new words. Sometimes we have to resort to just being with them and doing things they want done—but only, of course, if these actions represent the kind of service that is faithful to Jesus Christ.

"What we *can* do often depends on our past history. This is especially true with the Jews. This past history has been almost unbelievably awful! Most of us have only come to realize how bad it has been as a result of studies of the Holocaust. Now we realize that Christians have persecuted Jews through the centuries, and that we bear a lot of the guilt even for Nazi crimes against the Jews. We can't study this history without repenting. And part of that *metanoia,* turning around, means that we have to stop telling the Jews so many things and start listening to them. That means that we don't decide what they need; we ask them."

"I've read a little about pogroms and other Christian atrocities against the Jews," says Ms. McNutt, "so I think I understand you. Perhaps matters have been worse than I realized. I do see that right now is not a good time to witness to them about Jesus Christ. But is this just a tactical matter, or something more? With the Muslims, I understood you to say that the soft sell is tactical. We still hope they will become Christians someday. Are we just laying off on the Jews for a while, expecting to return to the task of evangelism as the situation changes?"

"That's an excellent question, Ms. McNutt, and I wish I knew the answer. The truth is that I am a very practical man. I know a lot about the history of missions and of the ecumenical movement, and I could tell you about a number of pronouncements and policy statements that have come out of recent discussions. Almost all of them, except from very conservative sects, back off from direct evangelism. I support that. But I don't know what will be the best Christian policy fifty years from now. I'm inclined to leave that to my successors."

Lois McNutt thanks Dr. Schmidt sincerely. She is really grateful. She had not thought about obeying the Great Commission in such practical and historically relative terms before. But it made sense. Blind obedience to commands, regardless of the circumstances and the probable consequences, is not her idea of being a good Christian. She sees that most of the churches have long recognized the importance of wise strategy and feels much better about what she had previously thought was her own inconsistency or failure to act on professed beliefs.

Still, she is not satisfied. Nothing Dr. Schmidt said helped her answer the question about the ultimate destiny of her Jewish friends. Are they saved through their faith, so that they have no need of Christ? Or does the Christian know that they need Christ but also that the past sins of Christians against Jews prevent them from speaking of Christ now?

Professor Schmidt does not think so much in those terms. But as Ms. McNutt is leaving, it occurs to him that one of his newer colleagues, Professor Lora Mae Wilkins, wrote her dissertation on Jewish-Christian relations in Antioch in the days of Chrysostom. No doubt Ms. McNutt would enjoy talking with her. When she agrees to his suggestion, he calls Wilkins and arranges a meeting for Ms. McNutt and her on Thursday morning.

3. Professor Wilkins—Church Historian

Lois McNutt does not know what to expect. For one thing, she realizes that her image of seminary professors is decidedly male. She is excited to meet a woman in that role. For another, she is going to talk with someone who has given focused attention to Jewish-Christian relations.

It would never have occurred to her that learning about Saint Chrysostom would be the way to delve into her questions about Christ and the Jews. Indeed, she does not remember that she has ever heard of Chrysostom before, so she looks him up in her encyclopedia. It turns out that he is considered one of the greatest preachers in Christian history and that his sermons are still studied. He lived in Antioch in the second half of the fourth century, and he preached against the Jews! That seems less promising, but she will go with an open mind to learn what Professor Wilkins has to say.

Professor Wilkins is quite excited, too. She has just joined the faculty of the seminary, having completed her dissertation the preceding year. She is preparing it now for publication. In limited academic circles, she has found some interest in her ideas, but this is the first time that anyone outside academia has wanted to talk with her about them. Wilkins selected the topic out of real concern about what had gone so wrong in the church in its relation to the Jews. The chance to talk with a layperson who saw the connection is refreshing.

When they meet, Ms. McNutt expresses her puzzlement. "Why did you choose to write about a Christian anti-Semite?"

Lora Mae Wilkins smiles. "Professor Schmidt described the dissertation so briefly that he gave you a wrong impression, I fear. I'm a church and social historian. We are not so much interested in the particular ideas of famous people as in what was going on in the church and society as a whole. Our best sources for Christian-Jewish relations in the late fourth century in Antioch are Chrysostom's sermons. From what he is denouncing, we can tell a lot about what was going on. We can relate that to other sources and put together a fairly reliable picture."

It is Ms. McNutt's turn to laugh at herself. "The truth is, I fear, that I have little idea about the kind of research you academics do. I certainly jumped to the wrong conclusion. In any case, I would like to learn something of what you found out. How were Christian-Jewish relations in those days?"

Wilkins answers enthusiastically, "One of the things that becomes clear is that lots of people in Antioch did not make a sharp distinction between Jews and Christians. They looked pretty much alike from a pagan point of view. Even among Jews and Christians themselves the separation had not gone very far. They mingled freely, and some of them even attended each other's services."

"So when we go back that far, we find a time when Christians had not yet begun to persecute Jews," responds Ms. McNutt. "That's good to hear."

"That's true," says Dr. Wilkins. "Although the situation is highly varied in different places, Christians as Christians did not begin to persecute non-Christians until they were well-established. But the seeds of future persecution were already there. The emperors were Christian and wanted Christianity to be a unifying force in the empire. That created problems for dissidents. And even more important, there was a tradition of anti-Jewish preaching and teaching in the church. Chrysostom stands in that tradition. For him the good relations between lay Christians and Jews were a source of worry. He wanted Christians to look down on Jews—and he was very influential."

"It bothers me," comments Ms. McNutt, "that we call a man with so much hostility to others a 'saint.' My ideas of saints are quite different. I guess love is the major element."

"It bothers me, too," Dr. Wilkins replies. "But the fact that Chrysostom preached against the Jews doesn't mean that he was a mean or cruel man. What we find again and again in history is that the people who care most about their own communities are often quite harsh in their condemnation of others. This is true especially when the other communities threaten theirs. Judaism in Antioch was quite attractive to a good many Christians. In defense of his church, Chrysostom wanted to persuade his people to avoid this temptation. The best way to do that was to depict the Jews in a bad light. No doubt, Chrysostom thought he was acting out of love. Perhaps he was."

"Does that mean that social rivalry was the basis for anti-Jewish teaching?" asks Ms. McNutt. "I had thought the problem was theological."

"We social historians don't make such a sharp distinction," Dr. Wilkins answers. "Certainly many of the arguments used to put the Jews down were theological. My view is that they were used for sociological purposes. We can predict that when one group feels threatened by another, it will say harsh things about the other. When we know enough about the belief system, we can make a pretty good guess just *what* they will say. But the *what* seems less important than the *that*. The results follow chiefly from the *that*."

Ms. McNutt decides there is time for one more question. "You have talked about Judaism's being attractive to lay Christians. Was the issue here again only the *that,* or were there particular things about Judaism that made it a special threat?"

"Well, I guess that Judaism was inherently more threatening than other social groups," answers Professor Wilkins. "Other groups could be viewed as those that had not yet been converted. The assumption was that the gospel of Jesus Christ carried such convincing power that all would yield before it. But it was hard to see the Jews that way. Christianity had arisen among them, so they should have understood it well. Yet they had rejected it, sometimes contemptuously.

"That continuing rejection was a threat to the ability of Christianity to be convincing. Christians had to explain this rejection to themselves in a way that did not discredit Christianity. The only way to do that was to depict the Jewish rejection in harsh colors, really demonic ones. The Jews rejected their Messiah and called down the responsibility for crucifying him on their own heads. They deserved whatever happened to them. In some ways the horrible teachings about Jews that have led to the Holocaust were inevitable, given the need of Christians to believe that the Jewish rejection of Jesus was completely unjustified. It is a sad business."

Yes, Lois thinks, as she gets up to leave, it *is* a sad business. She can't remember hearing such vicious attacks on the Jews in her church experience. But, yes, they were depicted as having been wrong in rejecting Jesus. She herself had assimilated ideas like that. *However much we try to respect them now,* she thinks, *we Christians inevitably feel that the Jews made a mistake in continuing on their way when Jesus came to them and gave himself for them.* She realizes that the term *Jew* evoked some negative feelings in her, even though she liked individual Jews so much. Being a part of the Christian community did make them "other," and an "other" who had inherently a negative relation to herself and her own community. Perhaps the sociological approach is the way to go!

4. Professor Atwater: New Testament

Lois McNutt goes home and thinks about this. But she still is not satisfied. She cannot see her beliefs *only* in sociological terms.

79

She really does believe that Jesus Christ is her Savior and Lord. And she thinks that he wants to be Savior and Lord for everyone. She still needs to know: Does that exclude his own people, the Jews? Surely that is not what the New Testament teaches!

There are two professors of New Testament at the seminary, and she cannot tell from their courses which one it is better to contact. Either of them, she feels sure, will be able to help her think about the issue. So far she has learned about the extent of the Christian crimes against the Jews and how Christians are trying to repent, and she has a better sense of how these crimes came about. But whether Jesus is the only savior is an issue that did not seem to fit in either conversation. She will ask a New Testament scholar straight out what some of the key texts mean.

She calls Professor Johnson, but since there is no answer, she calls Professor Atwater instead. He answers and agrees to see her. When his office door opens, Lois is inwardly startled to find that he is black. Again, her preconceived images! *But why not?* she thinks to herself. She explains to him a bit about her quest and about her conversations with Professors Schmidt and Wilkins.

Before she has a chance to ask her prepared question, Professor Atwater asks: "Did you realize that the competition between Christian and Jewish communities explains quite a few things in the New Testament also? The Gospel of John, especially, was written in a small Christian community keenly threatened, at least in its own self-respect, by the Jews. Obviously Jesus himself would never have talked about his own community in the way the Johannine Jesus speaks of the Jews. Some of what is placed on the lips of Jesus in that Gospel is really quite shocking. Imagine the real Jesus saying that the Jews are the children of the devil! The idea would be laughable if the historical consequences had not been so terrible."

Ms. McNutt is shocked. She knows that scholars do not suppose that everything in the New Testament is totally factual. She has even studied some of the Synoptics in parallel and has seen how what must have been the same event was reported differently in each. She knows that the Gospel of John is seen more as a meditation on Jesus than as a report on what he had actually said. But Dr. Atwater's tone went far beyond that. He seemed to be attacking the Gospel as vicious!

"I agree that that is a hard saying," she replies at length. "But the way you have spoken of it leaves me puzzled as to how you understand the authority of Scripture."

"I was a bit abrupt, wasn't I! Actually, I would not be nearly so upset by that passage if the Gospel of John did not have so much authority. You know that it is the most popular Gospel, often published all by itself, as if it were the epitome of Christian truth. Yet, in my view, unless it is read in the light of the context in which it was written and of what we know of the real Jesus, it can do more harm than good."

Ms. McNutt has come equipped with some of the New Testament passages attributing salvation only to Jesus. John's Gospel has contributed more than its share. She can see that Professor Atwater would make short work of her verses from that Gospel. She looks hastily at her list and selects a passage from Matthew (11:27). "The question I most want to ask you, Dr. Atwater, is how to understand the passages in the New Testament that make such strong and exclusive claims for Jesus Christ that it seems clear that no one can be saved except those who believe on him. I'm particularly concerned about what that means for the Jews. For example, here is a text from Matthew. Jesus says: 'All things have been handed over to me by my Father; and no one knows the Son except the Father, and no one knows the Father except the Son and anyone to whom the Son chooses to reveal him.' What do you make of that?"

Dr. Atwater replies soberly. "The first question we need to ask is Who said that? Because it is a canonized passage, we must deal with it seriously, whatever the answer to that question. But the original context affects the original meaning as well as our interpretation. Even with the Johannine passage of which I spoke so harshly, if we picture this as language used by an oppressed minority about the oppressor, it is not so offensive. Some of my fellow blacks talk about whites as 'white devils.' I don't approve, but I can certainly understand.

"Even in the Synoptics we have to distinguish between sayings that are authentic words of Jesus and those that arose in the early church. That is very difficult in many instances. Scholars have reached consensus on a good many sayings, but debate goes on with respect to others. The worst consequence of all this is that it

81

almost excludes laypeople from responsible interpretation of the Bible!

"Still, I think laypeople can make some useful judgments, too, even about this sort of technical scholarship. Look carefully at the verse you read me. There is a shift within the verse. In the first phrase, Jesus talks in the first person; after that he speaks quite objectively about himself. This language about *the Son* and *the Father* is very unlikely to be that of a Galilean teacher talking about himself and *his* Father. It sounds much more like the language of the church *about* Jesus and God."

"That does make sense," Ms. McNutt replies. "And I truly appreciate the care with which you have discussed the problem of New Testament scholarship. But you have already agreed that the words of Jesus are not the only sayings in the Bible that have authority in the Christian community. Some of the verses I brought with me are not even attributed to Jesus. Paul used some pretty strong language too!"

"You are quite right, Ms. McNutt. The question Who said what when? has preoccupied New Testament scholars a great deal. But the church sometimes belittles it. Some theologians say it makes no difference. The Bible is the witness to Christ, they say, and as such it has authority. Most of us biblical scholars think that way of putting it oversimplifies questions that need to be kept in view, but we do have to deal with all the passages. And many of them do speak of Christ as though there can be no way to salvation except through him."

"Then are we as Christians bound by that judgment?" This is Lois McNutt's real question, and she is glad that at last it has fit into a conversation.

"That is not really a question for us New Testament scholars," Dr. Atwater answers. "It is a question for the church. The church established the canon. The church attributes to the texts it has canonized whatever authority it wishes. But we New Testament scholars do make a contribution. We keep pointing out that there were many voices in the early church, that they do not all say the same thing. Asserting the authority of the Bible still doesn't tell us just what to believe.

"For my part, I incline to trust the authority of positive statements much more than negative ones. I mean, I have no doubt that Paul found himself transformed through Jesus Christ. I have no doubt that this was the experience of many early Christians. I also have no doubt that they rightly saw that the power of Christ to transform was not limited to one group of people. Christ saved both Jews and Gentiles, both slaves and free, both men and women. They were convinced Christ could save everyone.

"Sometimes, though, while they were making strong valid affirmations of the power of Christ for salvation, the language takes on a negative cast. It says that there is 'no other name.' It says that those who do not accept Christ are condemned. Now, that may seem to be just another way of saying the same thing, but I don't think so. So when I come across the passages that say what cannot happen, I don't trust them. I think people in those days, like people today, could get carried away by their rightful enthusiasm and wrongly deny that there is anything good except what has been so good for themselves. I'm now talking like a systematic theologian, not a New Testament scholar."

"I appreciate your doing that," Ms. McNutt assures him. "What you said is quite moving to me, and I will think differently about doctrines like this in the future. Is there anything more you can tell me about New Testament teaching about the Jews?"

"We haven't said anything about Romans 9–11," replies Dr. Atwater. "That is the *locus classicus* for this discussion. Paul did not just lump Jews and unconverted Gentiles together as non-Christians, as some people have done in later times. The relation of Christianity to Judaism is quite distinct. And for Paul, that does not mean only that Christianity grew out of Judaism. It also means that we are destined to come together in the end. Paul reconciled himself to the fact that, for the time being, most of his fellow Jews did not accept Christ. He clearly objected to attitudes of superiority in relation to these Jews on the part of the Gentile Christians."

"Thanks, Dr. Atwater, I was so preoccupied with the one question of whether Christ is the only savior that I had given no thought to Paul's own reflections about the Jews. I'm not sure just what they mean to me, but this is one more step in freeing me from posing the question so simplistically. You've been a great help!"

5. Professor Reynolds: Systematic Theology

On the way home, Ms. McNutt suddenly thinks of what
Professor Atwater had said about systematic theology. Perhaps
the question she is asking is most directly of all a question of
systematic theology. She had been intimidated by that label, but
she liked the comments Dr. Atwater had made when he put on
that hat. When she gets home, she calls Professor James
Reynolds, the seminary's systematician. He, too, expresses
willingness to see her and his sincere pleasure at the prospect.

Dr. Reynolds smiles when Ms. McNutt tells him what Dr.
Atwater had said about being out of his field when he made
comments about biblical authority. Reynolds knows well the
tendency of his colleagues to disown responsibility for taking a
position on strictly theological issues, in spite of the fact that so
much of what they said was laden with theological importance.

"One of my favorite theologians," he tells Ms. McNutt, "said
something similar to Dr. Atwater in a little different way.
H. Richard Niebuhr, in a marvelous little book called *The Meaning
of Revelation,* says that as Christians our task is to confess what
Jesus Christ means to us. As in Dr. Atwater's case, that is entirely
positive. Our confession says nothing about what other people
cannot find or have not found in other ways. We ask them to
listen to our confession, and in turn we need to listen to theirs.

"I think that is a very good way to approach people who are not
Christian. We are not saying they are saved or that they are not
saved. *They* tell *us* about who and what they are. But we do witness
to the power of Jesus Christ to save. We can do that with
conviction and authenticity because we know Christ's power in
the lives of people in our own community. We commend Christ to
others. But we also listen to what they share with us."

"Does that mean that I should talk about Christ with my Jewish
friends?" Lois McNutt wants to know.

"Ideally, I think it does," responds Dr. Reynolds. "But I'm sure
that Dr. Schmidt talked about how the mainline denominations
have given up every form of mission to the Jews. The problem is
that Jews have felt so much pressure from us for so long that *any*
testimony to Christ on our part feels to them like a threat. As a

84

matter of practical advice, I would suggest that you encourage your friends to talk about what Judaism means to them, and that you listen very openly and appreciatively. *If* at some point they want to know what Christianity means to you, don't hold back, but be very careful to make it a personal confessional statement of *your* experience. It would be a mistake, I think, even to hope that this would cause them to leave their synagogue to join your church. After losing six million Jews to Hitler, the Jewish community dreads losing any more to the church."

"But in that case, what is the point of witnessing at all—or confessing as you call it?" Ms. McNutt asks.

"My answer to that is just my own," says Dr. Reynolds slowly. "It has developed in my reflections about Romans 9–11. I share Paul's hope that someday Jews and Gentiles will be reunited. The Jews' road to Christ will not be ours. It will be their own. It will be through their own reflection on their own tradition that they will someday reappropriate the Christ we took away from them. The main contribution we can make to this process is to leave them alone. But I think that within the context of friendship, and as an expression of that friendship, we can help them appreciate the greatest figure in their own history: Jesus. Loyalty to Jesus has been used against them, as a slogan justifying persecution. It is hard for them to view Jesus openly after that. But when they really understand that the deepest meaning of Jesus has been so positive for the world, that will increase their interest in reappropriating him for themselves. They won't stop being Jews, but their Judaism will be fulfilled."

Lois McNutt is moved by this. She almost feels that her quest is complete. She can continue to believe in the universality of the salvation effected in Jesus Christ without disowning the integrity of her full acceptance of her Jewish friends in their Jewishness. But she is not sure she can confess her faith in Christ in quite the nonthreatening way Dr. Reynolds proposed.

"What you say sounds great," she comments. "But one point troubles me. You talk of the Jews accepting Jesus, but it sounds more like accepting a historical figure than like accepting Jesus as God. I don't think I can confess to what Jesus Christ means to me without using language that will offend my Jewish friends, however hard I try to avoid that. Isn't there finally the question: Was Jesus God or not? If Jews agreed that Jesus was God, would they still be Jews?"

"I guess the truth is that I don't myself like the language you have just used. To me it sounds different from anything I find in the New Testament, and that language already goes a long way in exalting Jesus. Some of the creeds come closer to saying that, but actually they avoid it too, at least in such a one-sided way. If you want to be orthodox, then if you say that Jesus was God, in the next breath you must say that Jesus was completely human. That differentiates Jesus from God, since of God we will not say the same thing.

"My own preference in language is different. We Christians do confess that in Jesus God was incarnate. That can be supported from the New Testament in a number of ways, beginning with the first chapter of John. But that chapter makes it clear that Jesus is not the only place in the world that the Word who is God is present. Becoming flesh is different, no doubt, from being present in life and in thinking. Exactly how it is different we are not told. But it is surely continuous with it, as well.

"We are back to where we started with Richard Niebuhr. We can confess that God is incarnate in Jesus Christ. It is not for us to make negative statements about how God is absent to others. We can say that from our point of view Christ is present in all in some way. Nor can we say just what the difference is between God's presence to us as incarnate in Jesus and God's presence in Word and Spirit to Old Testament Jews, or later Jews either, for that matter. I trust the Jews, and I believe that when they have reappropriated Jesus they can teach us something about these matters."

This is more than Lois McNutt is ready to appropriate herself. She does sense that when any Christian doctrine is explored in greater depth, it loses the crude simplicity with which one begins. The either/ors that trouble the Christian when confronted with some doctrinal demand give way to more nuanced views that do not necessarily carry the same disturbing consequences. Biblical scholars work on this in their way, and theologians in theirs. She will work on it in her own way.

DOING YOUR THEOLOGY

1. What is your own position on the question that is troubling Ms. McNutt? How do you argue for it?
2. Do the contributions of the four professors help you in clarifying the issues or coming to a conclusion? Explain in detail.
3. Analyze the views of the four scholars in relation to the Wesleyan quadrilateral discussed in chapter 4.

CHAPTER SIX

Professionals

HELP AND HINDRANCE

1. Where Professionals Can Help

*T*he theological work described and illustrated in the first four chapters is almost impossible to do all alone. We need to talk things through, get suggestions, try them on for size, discard them, and try others. Thinking of all the possibilities alone and then working out good tests is more than most of us expect of ourselves. That does not mean we can't do quite a lot even if no one else is interested. But it does mean that working with others is a lot more fun and more promising. Christianity, after all, is a community movement; we need each other.

Chapter 5 illustrated another kind of help, that of professionals. A professional could also be a fellow searcher in the quest for a better theology. That would be fine. But chapter 5 depicted a woman who knew enough about what professionals do that she could turn to them for help. Remember in chapter 1 the analogy of taking responsibility for your own health? You can take care of your own health in many ways, but you also need professional help. You need to know enough about professionals to make good judgments about whose help you require and when you require it. Your theological health must be treated in the same way.

Why do you need professional help at all? Basically the answer is that although doing good theology is not primarily dependent on objective knowledge, there are severe limits to what you can do without it. You can to some extent, of course, do your own scholarship. For example, you can read the Bible by yourself. But many questions come up along the way that a professional can answer easily, and the nonprofessional hardly at all.

This is not to take back anything that has been said. It is not proposing that you ask the professional to do your work for you. *You* have to figure out what *you* believe. That is the bottom line. But that is no reason not to get all the help you can; seeking the help of others may help you clarify your own ideas.

In chapter 2, the character Henry Smith gave several justifications of his position that homosexual acts are always wrong, but I may have attributed to him more arguments than he would have come up with on his own. For example, I had him recognize and explore the relevance of natural law theory, and then I brought in a bit of anthropology and psychology.

On the other hand, many laypeople do have information about natural law theory, anthropology, and psychology. These are all part of public discourse, and not specialized theological information. Some laypeople have professional expertise in these fields well beyond mine or that of professional theologians in general. Being "lay" in the church does not mean one is lay in regard to all professions. There is nothing particularly artificial about including information of this kind in tracing through a lay Christian's reasoning.

Many of you have college degrees. You have had a lot of exposure to professionals in many fields. You know what to expect of sociologists, chemists, and psychologists. You know where to look, or to whom you need to talk, if your questioning leads in those directions. You know how to use the local library and get help from a reference librarian. The examples in the first four chapters used only information that is accessible to you in normal ways. This chapter is not about that kind of professional help.

But even many college graduates, even those who are Christians, have little idea what professional theologians are like and how they can help. There are two types of assistance that laypeople can expect from professional theologians.

First, professional theologians have a wide background of information about what theology has been. This frees them from being bound by the meaning of "theology" in popular church usage today. It also enables them to talk about what is going on in theological thinking in distinction from the theological ideas themselves.

Second, professional theologians can contribute information and insights. Chapter 5 illustrated this. The professors with whom Ms. McNutt talked contributed historical information about Christian anti-Judaism. They also suggested ways in which Christians can think about their faith and about Judaism. They could do this because they had specialized knowledge and experience. Some of them were familiar with the way in which other thinkers have dealt with the question, and they have bases for judging the effectiveness of these approaches rarely available to those who are not specialists.

Although professionals are likely to have knowledge and experience not equally available to laypeople, there is no fixed boundary between the two groups. Aspects of understanding that arise in the professional community, whether in medicine, psychology, biology, or theology, pass over into the lay discussion. One of the ways of stating the problem this book addresses is that so little of the work of theologians in recent times has passed over into lay discussion in the old-line churches. Only if all Christians take responsibility for their own theology will this situation change. The hope is that the boundary between lay and professional knowledge will shift, so that much of what, realistically, can be attributed today only to the professional will be part of the lay theological discussion.

One of the convictions that I expressed in chapter 3 is that there is no theologically neutral way to discuss doing theology. In chapter 4, I argued that experience, reason, tradition, and Scripture are radically interconnected. You cannot appeal to any one without involving all four. I believe that if you become serious about theology, you will discover the truth of these ideas for yourself, but I also believe that certain obstacles to doing theology will be removed if you learn in advance, from a professional, what to expect.

But there is one thing *not* to expect. You cannot expect the professional to have the *answers*. Some professionals have worked out provisional answers for themselves. Some have not even done that. The ones who have their own answers can share them, just as any Christian can. They may be well thought through and tested. If so, they carry a measure of authority. But not all experts agree on all answers. You can always find another professional who has thought just as responsibly with just as much information and has come to a different position. Expert authority cannot make decisions for you!

2. University and Seminary Professors

The real question in becoming a good theologian is not what you can do by yourself or in discussion with other laypeople. The real goal is to become as good a theologian as possible, getting help wherever you can find it. Professional theologians are an important—and available—source of help. You need to know who they are and what they can contribute, as well as what they cannot do.

Most professional theologians are professors in theological schools. That's almost the only place people get paid to be theological scholars. This chapter will focus on these professors. But other people, such as pastors and university professors of religion, can provide information.

Pastors have spent some time with seminary professors and know a lot about them. They know what these professors can contribute and what they can't. They know what to expect to find in their books and where to look for them.

In addition, pastors are professionals themselves. They are not paid to do research, and in their busy lives, they have little time for that. But they are expected to have worked through some ranges of problems and to be able to build bridges between scholars and laypeople. As you seek professional help, begin with your pastor. You will soon discover how much your pastor can help you with specific questions.

The other important source of professional help on theological matters is to be found in liberal arts colleges and in universities, especially in those that have departments of religion. Today, the work of a lot of people teaching in colleges and universities is quite similar to that of the professors in seminaries.

The main difference in the two groups is that professionals in seminaries are urged to think about how their studies are related

91

to the Christian faith and to the church, especially to the role of the pastors. Those who deal with similar topics in the university are likely to raise this question much less. Some even conscientiously avoid it. They want their work to have all the objectivity and detachment of university scholarship in general.

Sometimes you may seek information that can be provided just as well by a scholar in the secular university as by one in the theological seminary. But sometimes the seminary professor is a better bet. Professors in seminaries *expect* to deal with Christians thinking about their faith. In the departments of religion, some do and some do not.

Thus far, all the professors of theology have been grouped together. Actually, they are divided into specialties. Even within the specialties there are subspecialties. You could have some needs that almost any seminary professor could meet. But many times, questions to one professor will be referred to a colleague.

Within the seminary, the professional specialties to which you are most likely to turn are the Old Testament, the New Testament, church history, systematic theology, Christian ethics, ecumenics, and missions. You may have to go to the university to find a professor of the history of religions. Sometimes a professor of preaching, pastoral care, or Christian education will have your answer.

Most of the help you will get from seminary professors will be through their writings. Your pastor will often be able to direct you to appropriate writings. If a church group strives to become good theologians, you can read different books or articles and share results. But even for such purposes, you would do well to understand a bit more about who these professors are and how they think. Hence, the story told in chapter 5 of a layperson's experience with seminary professors may be suggestive of what can be expected from books as well as from lectures and personal conversations.

3. Evaluating the Professors

In the story in chapter 5, we met four professors, all fictional, but not untypical. Each could contribute something. Dr. Schmidt, the professor of ecumenics and missions, had been immersed in the church's mission and reflection about it. He knew well the official positions adopted by the several denominations as well as their practices. If he had a definite theological position of his own, he did not offer it. Perhaps if the conversation had been in another context, one in which he was not addressed in terms of his professional competence, he might have shared his own struggle to understand. But we cannot make this assumption. Just as many clergy and laity do not have clear theological convictions of their own, so it is also with many professors in schools of theology. For many of them, the professional expertise for which they are employed is something that requires specialized knowledge about the church and its beliefs and practices. It does not require reflective convictions of their own.

The social historian, Professor Wilkins, clearly had convictions. She was convinced that it is important to understand our shared heritage. She believed that the important heritage is not limited to institutional history and the ideas and deeds of a few leaders. She was also convinced that Christian treatment of Jews throughout history is deplorable and that the church needs to understand how this underside of its life came about and is perpetuated today. But she did not take it as her responsibility to work out the normative form of Christian teaching for the present. Nor did she feel the need to examine whether and how these convictions arise out of her personal faith in Jesus Christ. Again, in a different context she might have been willing to reflect on these matters, to share her own theological struggles. But she did not think of this as belonging in her dissertation or in her classroom, and it played no role in her conversation with Ms. McNutt.

It is more difficult for New Testament scholars such as Dr. Atwater to maintain this kind of distance from theology. The interpretation of the New Testament has immediate theological implications. The authority of the texts is a question that biblical scholars cannot avoid altogether. Their method of studying the Bible already has presuppositions that are in tension with some views of the Bible's nature and authority. Yet even here a line is typically drawn. Like professors of New Testament, scholars are apt to refuse responsibility for deciding just what contemporary believers should make of the results of critical historical and literary inquiry. At some point they are likely to defer to their colleagues in systematic theology, although they are also likely to disagree with what these theologians say and consider it insufficiently informed by biblical scholarship.

Directly answering theological questions is the specific task of systematic theology. Ideally these answers would be informed by the practical and theoretical knowledge of all the other faculty members. In fact, of course, professors of systematic theology will have only a lay understanding of much of what their colleagues teach. Their own specialized knowledge is likely to be primarily of what other theologians have taught and are now teaching. Indeed, some professors of systematic theology would not have answered Ms. McNutt out of their personal reflection. They would have told her what Karl Barth and Paul Tillich and Wolfhart Pannenberg and Jürgen Moltmann had to say on the topic. If pressed for their own views, they might have expressed these in terms of critical reflection on one or another of the theologians they described.

In the story, the systematic theologian, Dr. Reynolds, was the last scholar interviewed by Ms. McNutt. However, the results were left open-ended. The theologian's criticism of the doctrine that Jesus is God drew on views of the Bible and church history, especially the teaching of the great creeds. His ideas could be tested in further discussion with scholars in those fields. Ms. McNutt, in the process of developing her own theology, has no reason to accept the views of any one systematic theologian as normative or decisive. She should treat them as suggestions and proposals for her to test both in relation to historical information and in relation to her own deepest convictions.

In the story, Professor Reynolds spoke out of his own struggle to understand. He referred to others only as they helped him come to his conclusions. Ms. McNutt could have asked him to direct her to other theologians with different proposals. Knowing more of the options being explored by other well-informed and thoughtful Christians would increase her freedom to develop her convictions.

On the other hand, there is a danger of being overwhelmed. As we realize how much relevant history there is, and how many and complex are the ways that contemporary thinkers have responded to the issues, we may decide that we have no right to any opinion at all! This is understandable but disastrous.

It has had inimical consequences for the theological faculties themselves. Even though they are called "faculties of theology," the truth is, as we have seen, that they consist of a group of specialists most of whom decline to accept professional responsibility for their own theologies. Each member of the faculty has an area of expertise defined, in most cases, by a particular subject matter. Certain methods have been developed in the scholarly community for the study of these subject matters. The application of these methods to these subject matters constitutes their academic disciplines.

Of course, the question of which disciplines should be taught to those studying for ministry determines the selection of faculty. But the kind of research done by the faculty member and the way the subject matter is taught are largely determined by the more or less autonomous development of the academic discipline. This development leads to greater and greater specialization. For example, the social history of the early church can constitute such a specialization. Someone who is highly competent in that may know very little either about the social history of the Reformation or about the philosophical theologies developed by leading thinkers of the early church. A systematic theologian may be well-versed in twentieth-century theological developments in central Europe but know very little about African-American theology or feminist theology as they have emerged in the United States.

The result is that it is difficult for a small faculty to provide prospective ministers with an overview of the Bible, the history of Christianity, and theology. The result is also that the importance for actual ministry of what is studied is often obscured. And finally, the result is that a seminary education, instead of encouraging prospective pastors to become theologians, may intimidate them. Most of their professors do not claim to be theologians themselves. The impression is given that to do responsible theological work, they would need all the information provided collectively by the faculty, and perhaps more besides. But professors do not model the integration asked of students. One reason that so few pastors make serious efforts to be good theologians is that the task appears impossible to them. Inevitably, some of this attitude is communicated to laypeople as well.

I have written this book to counteract this development. All of us, laypeople, ministers, and professors, simply as Christians, *are* theologians. The task is to become better ones. Despite the time and attention we devote to this task, none of us, not even the professionally systematic theologians, will arrive at final conclusions. But the fact that we can, at best, engage in a constant search does not minimize the value of that search. We *can* clarify, purify, and deepen our convictions.

4. A Word of Advice

The practical purpose of these two chapters is to suggest what help you as a lay theologian can get from professional scholars, especially those in seminaries. But if taken too straightfowardly, the proposals are not very practical. Most of you will not be able to interview four professors. If there were a sudden burst of interest on your part, the small number of professionals in this field would be quickly overwhelmed.

The real point is to suggest what is available in books. The truly practical approach for you is to talk with your pastor about books that would help you think through your most pressing concern.

But far better than pursuing your interests alone would be joining a group to work with the pastor. The task of reading relevant materials can be shared. Also, only as you articulate your emerging views and get critical feedback are they likely to mature.

A group could study the Christian view of Judaism to gain all the ideas offered in the previous chapter and, indeed, to find a basis for moving toward shared conclusions. If its members cannot agree on the conclusions, they may at least clarify the points of difference and the reasons for these differences. Laypeople who do this are becoming mature theologians.

Or a group could study the implications of feminism for Christian theology by familiarizing themselves with the most relevant literature. They could well begin with the practical issue of the use of feminine imagery in worship that was introduced in chapter 1. Again, they might not come to agreement, but they may certainly move toward a responsible analysis of why and how they disagree. In the process, they may consider many fundamental theological issues. These laypeople are also becoming serious theologians.

Although it is not practical for each layperson to interview four professors, it is not unrealistic to think that professors would welcome the opportunity to talk with groups engaged in serious theological reflection based on study. These encounters would be of greatest value at advanced stages of work together.

This partnership between laypeople in local churches and professors in seminaries would mark a new day in the life of old-line denominations. As the number of lay theologians increased, the understanding of the role of the pastor would change, and that would affect the self-understanding of the seminaries as well. But most of all, lay leadership of the churches would be renewed in a fully responsible way, and the church would once again make its decisions on reflective Christian grounds.

The negative side of the strong emergence of lay theology is that serious theological differences might become more explicit and more keenly felt. For example, some who have acquiesced in the cessation of any evangelical mission to the Jews might become deeply convinced that this must be renewed, whereas others would feel strongly that Christians as Christians have no business trying to convert individual Jews away from their synagogues. The division of opinion on using feminine language about God might become more intense.

In general, many might discover that those with whom they most agree are members of other denominations. There might be tendencies to redraw denominational boundaries on lines of current theological issues rather than on those of an earlier period. Institutional appeals for loyalty might become less effective. It is not hard to see why some people with institutional responsibilities lack zeal for a revival of serious lay theology.

But the negative consequences of such a revival are only the intensification of what is happening anyway. Denominational loyalty based on old issues has worn thin. Since denominations now stand for very little, people with serious commitments often drift away, finding fellowship where they can. Our national bodies are torn by issues of the sort discussed here.

There is no assurance that lay theology will put an end to these divisions. But there *is* the possibility that those of us who study these issues seriously as *Christians* will understand one another and respect one another more than at present. We may be able to define together what a denomination *can* do with the enthusiastic support of thoughtful and informed laypeople. If new alignments are ultimately inevitable, a revival of lay theology may make it possible for this to occur without rancor and mutual contempt.

In any case, we really have no Christian alternative. To drift on into institutionalism with most Christians having little understanding of what is being lost in the process is not a viable choice. Faith in Christ requires our attempts to understand what faith entails. This is not an impossible task. We must try it.

DOING YOUR THEOLOGY

1. In your responses to earlier chapters, have you needed information or ideas that were not readily accessible to you in order to strengthen, clarify, correct, or advance your thinking? Specify some of them. In which instances, if any, would a professional theological scholar be able to help you? Can you specify what type of scholar would help you the most?

2. Can you find articles or books on your own, written by such scholars, that provide the information you need? If not, can your pastor, or someone else, help you to do so? Identify and evaluate the articles and books you have read. After securing the kind of assistance needed, rewrite your argument. Have your conclusions been affected by gaining this information from an outside source?

CHAPTER SEVEN

Christian Counterattack

1. The Long Retreat

*I*f we study the history of theology, we cannot help being struck by the way its range of topics has narrowed. For early church leaders, such as St. Augustine and St. Thomas Aquinas, no topic is excluded. They assumed that there is a Christian way of viewing everything. They talked about the history of the world and cosmology as well as politics and economics.

For them, all of this is in one sense talk about God and how God is incarnate in Jesus Christ. That is because God is actively involved in everything that happens. Through God's creative, redemptive work culminating in Jesus Christ, we are given insights into how every aspect of life is to be lived and every aspect of nature and history is to be understood.

This did not mean that every bit of information the Christian needs is to be derived from the Bible. Both Augustine and Thomas Aquinas made extensive use of the knowledge amassed by the Greeks. But their Christian convictions determined the way they interpreted and used this knowledge.

Neither Augustine nor Thomas Aquinas belittled the capacity of the human mind to think and understand. Both of them reasoned and argued brilliantly. They are studied in histories of philosophy as well as of theology. But neither thought that there could be a sphere for purely secular thought from which Christian thinking was excluded. Since God is Creator and Lord of all, faith in God relates believers to everything. Christian thinking and Christian practice similarly relate to everything.

The Protestant reformers Luther and Calvin continued this tradition. Indeed, they thought that earlier theologians had yielded too much to secular modes of thought by incorporating Greek philosophy in their theologies. They appealed to Scripture more exclusively as the source of understanding for whatever issues they encountered in the church or in the wider society.

Nevertheless, the breakup of the unity of western Christendom to which they contributed did pave the way for the rise of secularism. In particular, the religious persecutions and wars led many thoughtful and sensitive people to believe that the sphere of religion should be circumscribed. It seemed that as long as each theology made totalistic claims, believers in different theologies could not live peacefully together. It was necessary to differentiate those beliefs needed for a livable society from those on which differences could be tolerated. It would then be possible to have a secular state that allowed for religious diversity among its citizens.

Politically and socially, this liberal political solution has worked fairly well. In this country we take it for granted. We Christians give it strong support. We do not want any one institution, committed to any one theology, to control our public life.

This political shift from church-dominated society to secular society has benefited the churches themselves. When the church exercises great political power and has great social prestige, it attracts to its leadership persons who hunger for such power and prestige. Many of these people are also sincere Christians, but motives are likely to be mixed. Even when church leadership exercises much less power and has much less prestige, the motives of those who seek it are impure. We know that no social arrangement overcomes our sinfulness. But commitment to Christ is likely to play a much larger role when worldly rewards are less.

When the church does not exercise dominating power, it is in far better position to criticize those who do from a Christian perspective. This can, of course, be done irresponsibly, and the church can be wrong about what Christ calls us to do. It often fails to exercise the prophetic role and speaks more for the interests and prejudices of its most influential members. Nevertheless, with all its ambiguities, the record of denominational and ecumenical pronouncements on public matters is one in which we can take pride.

Nevertheless, there have been serious losses as well as gains. Christians have gradually reduced the range of topics about which they have thought *as Christians.* One by one the sciences have arisen and declared their autonomy. On the whole, Christians have granted this autonomy. Each time this happens, another area of thought is declared off limits to theology. The way Christians think about the world has been shaped more and more by the discoveries of these autonomous sciences and less and less by a distinctively Christian perspective.

Conservative Christians have resisted this theological retreat. The issue came to a head in the late nineteenth century over the evolutionary understanding of the world and especially of the emergence of human beings. The conservative Christian argument was often narrowly biblicist, insisting that the first chapter of Genesis must guide all our thought about origins. But more was at stake. Evolutionary doctrine involved a radical change in world-view, and this was being imposed on Christians by an autonomous science that denied any influence of Christianity.

Progressive Christians dealt with this crisis in two ways. Some undertook to bring their theistic faith to bear in the interpretation of the evidence in favor of evolution. They accepted evolution but offered a Christian interpretation. Others, however, adopted a dualistic position. They argued that there is a deep and fundamental difference between the human world and the natural world. Theology, they said, belongs only to the human world. Theories about the natural world are of no importance or interest to it.

If this acceptance of limits for Christian thinking omitted only the natural sciences, perhaps it would not affect Christian faith very seriously. But the line could not be drawn there. In earlier chapters, we saw how social sciences have also declared their autonomy. The same is true of psychology and history. The sphere in which Christians are free to speak as Christians has shrunk drastically. As a result, the action of Christians in society is informed more by our understanding of the world as given to us through these autonomous sciences than by our faith.

Theology in this context has become one academic discipline

alongside others. Its major topics are the interpretation of the Bible, the study of the history of Christianity, and the effort to formulate plausible views about God, Christ, the church, and Christian experience and morality. In other words, instead of studying the world and all the issues of life from the perspective of faith, theology is limited to studying Christianity itself. Much of its effort is devoted to clarifying what it is doing and how this activity is justified at all. In all this work it employs points of view and methods that come from the secular disciplines. Its results are often of only marginal interest to the Christian community.

Overall, then, Christian faith has been marginalized in the wider society, and theology has been marginalized among Christians. The previous chapters have described how the marginalization of theology among Christians can be ended. We can all recognize that we are already theologians and we can all become better ones. We saw that this cannot take place while we divide our loyalties between Christianity and other authorities. Unless our self-identification as Christians is primary, we cannot become good theologians.

Does this mean that those Christians who oppose the results of the autonomous sciences are right when these sciences conflict with the straightforward authority of biblical texts? Should we all support the "creationists" in their opposition to the teaching of evolution? I do not think so. I have proposed that we find within our faith ample reason to accept the evidence that the sciences uncover. Our Christian beliefs must do justice to this evidence. Few impartial observers believe that this is true of creationism. Trying to generate a biology or a physics or an astronomy or a psychology from biblical sources is a fruitless and mistaken task. The dualists are correct that this information about the natural world is not what the Bible is all about.

2. Reengaging the World

We Christians have often thought that the choice is either to defend explicit and literal biblical teaching against the autonomous sciences or to let the sciences determine how we think with regard to their topics. In fact, for the most part, we have adopted the second course. This has led to a drastic limitation of the direct role of faith in shaping our lives.

102

In chapter 3, we talked about how this direct role of faith can be supplemented by an indirect role. Roger Schwartz, the businessman who resented his pastor's preaching on economic issues, might believe that his affirmation of contemporary economic theory is a responsible Christian commitment. In this way, he can maintain his Christian integrity while rejecting much of what the Bible says about the pursuit of wealth.

The position of our oldline denominations seems to be generally of this sort. They do not dispute the authority of economic theory. As a result, they must accept the positive role of self-interest in economic life. They limit their pronouncement on the economy to matters of public policy on which economists themselves disagree. Some economists argue that in the long run society is better off if we do all we can to stimulate the growth of production and thus of market activity, even if that means allowing the poor to suffer in the meantime. Others argue that government should be concerned with those who are not successful in market competition and do what it can to meet their needs even if this slows market growth. Oldline churches generally side with the latter group, although many Christians do not agree with this policy. Indeed, conservative Christians are often found on the side of those who want government to play a minimal role even if that means the suffering of the poor. They sometimes incline to the view that meeting the needs of the poor should be left to private charity.

This is an important debate. The quality of life for many people now and in the future hinges on its outcome. But is this the only way in which Christians should engage in the discussion of the economy?

In the late nineteenth century and the early twentieth century there was another, more fundamental, debate among economists. This was the debate about the respective merits of capitalism and socialism. Christians entered into this debate as well. Again they were divided, just as were the economists. Socialist ideas appealed to Christians because they expressed concern for the poor who were suffering acutely under capitalism. Socialism was attractive also because it called people to work for the good of the whole community rather than out of pure self-interest.

103

But insofar as socialist practice entailed restriction of personal freedom and responsibility, most Christians opposed it. There was also the question as to whether government ownership of the means of production would lead to efficient use of resources. Many economists and Christians doubted this, and events have justified these doubts. As a result, despite the appeal of socialist motivations, few Christians in the United States today support socialist theory.

The fact that Christians who once supported socialism have, for the most part, abandoned this ideology, has further weakened the tendency of Christians to engage economics at a theoretical level. The victory of free market economic thought seems to be almost complete. The orthodox experts are vindicated. Christians feel that they must limit their involvement to policy issues that do not challenge the science of economics. Yet the cost to Christians is very large. It entails that Christians accept the desirability that much of public life be based on principles that are profoundly at variance with their ethical views.

The connection between this retreat and the near disappearance of lay theology is apparent. Lay Christians lead most of their lives outside the church as institution. They are thinking chiefly about matters related to their secular work. There was a time when thinking about one's work evidently involved Christian faith. But we have seen how this has become less and less true.

I have shown in earlier chapters how there are still many issues in which lay Christians have an interest that involve theological convictions. But the exclusion of the issues related to their work is a major limitation. Is this exclusion the last word on this matter?

My conviction is that it need not be and should not be. We should not choose between trying to impose biblicist ideas on science, on the one side, and simply accepting the existing form of each science as authoritative, on the other. There is a better option. The kind of thinking that we need to do as we become better theologians is relevant to critical thinking about the sciences as well.

This thinking can be done best by those who understand these sciences from within. But it is not done best by those who are fully socialized into the several disciplines. For example, a sociologist who thinks only as a sociologist is not in the best position to be critical of the discipline of sociology as a whole.

Christians who are involved in sociology and its conclusions but who have ideas and values that derive from their faith are in an excellent position to be critical. If they have learned to be critical of their own beliefs along the lines I have discussed, they can also be critical of beliefs generally assumed by sociologists. To be critical does not always mean to object. Sometimes criticism leads to reaffirmation. But it does not always do so. The results of the criticism of assumptions may lead to the adoption of different ones with new implications for sociological theory and research.

I am calling this approach a counterattack. After centuries of retreat before the rise of autonomous secular disciplines, I believe it is time that lay Christians become critical of the assumptions that underlie these disciplines. The purpose of such counterattack is not at all to subordinate these disciplines to the authority of the church. On the contrary, it should enable the disciplines to fulfill their intentions better.

Nevertheless, the critique may also change the nature of the disciplines and their relation to each other. Many people, both Christians and others, deplore the fragmentation of the disciplines as they are taught in our universities. Criticizing the assumptions developed autonomously in each may help to relate them to one another more effectively as well as to make them more compatible with fundamental Christian convictions.

Changes of this sort are not likely to be welcomed by all. We Christians are accustomed to understanding that all our beliefs are subject to judgment, that we are all creatures whose thinking is distorted. Only in God is there the final truth. But this self-relativizing habit of mind is not so influential within the academic disciplines. They are, of course, constantly correcting and improving their hypotheses and theories. But their more fundamental assumptions are rarely reconsidered. To criticize them is often felt as an attack on the discipline itself and on those who devote themselves to its advancement.

3. Institutional Criticism

The basic institutions of society emancipated themselves from the influence of Christianity more slowly than the sciences and academic disciplines. I mentioned above how the nation state did so in order that there could be toleration of more than one community of faith. The marketplace became independent during the same period. Most aspects of the medical system have been autonomous for a long time. Legal systems have sought autonomous grounds as well. Educational systems have had a long and complex history in this respect, but today they are largely autonomous, at least in this country.

This process of secularization of society's basic institutions has been influenced by the autonomy of the sciences and disciplines, but it has been less clear in its theoretical assumptions. Nevertheless, practice in each institution does express such assumptions. This is particularly true in the legal system where arguments must be given for basic decisions.

Analysis of the arguments given for Supreme Court decisions, for example, often makes the assumptions on which the decisions are made quite evident. These vary from justice to justice and from court to court. Some assumptions are quite acceptable to Christians; others are not. Christians can and should engage in this discussion.

But there is another level of assumptions operative within our legal system that is less often articulated. This underlies the system of courts and prisons as a whole. It expresses itself in our jury system, our differentiation of civil and criminal law, the adversarial relation between lawyers for defense and prosecution, the treatment of the victims of crimes, the treatment of criminals, the parole system, and in many other aspects of our legal system. The assumptions operative here are not always clear or consistent. I am making no judgment as to whether they are acceptable from a Christian point of view. I *am* asserting that making these assumptions conscious and evaluating them could be an important Christian contribution to the whole of our society.

The critique of institutions is closely related to that of disciplines. There are academic disciplines of jurisprudence and penology, for example, that both describe and justify what occurs within the legal system. Within them some explication and critique of assumptions already occurs.

As academic disciplines these have their own assumptions. These may not be the same as those that actually underlie the legal system. Sorting out these relations is also a worthwhile task.

Christians can earn the right to engage in such criticisms by criticizing first the assumptions that underlie their own institution—the church and its ordinary life. In fact, this criticism is unusually far advanced. It is because Christians have a tradition of self-criticism that they have the ability and the credentials to share in the criticism of other institutions and ideas.

The assumption-criticism for which I am calling is, or should become, a central part of lay theology. Professional theologians are, on the whole, inadequately immersed in these other institutions and insufficiently familiar with these other disciplines to provide the leadership needed. As you become skilled in analyzing and improving the assumptions that underlie your practice within the church and your moral judgments, you prepare yourself for this counterattack against the secularism that has so restricted the relevance of Christian faith.

4. Selecting Examples

The discussion above is quite abstract. As elsewhere in this book, I want to get beyond this abstraction by providing illustrations of how the critique of assumptions can take shape. But illustrations must be highly selective.

As my chief example, I select the discipline of economics. A case could be made for other selections, but I believe that this one is of special importance today. Among the social sciences, economics has the greatest prestige. Indeed, its methods are being extended to other social sciences because of their unusual success. The work of economists has direct effect on the self-understanding of business people and also on public policy. The tension between these effects and Christian values is unusually sharp. Furthermore, globally speaking, economic considerations now take precedence over all others in the shaping of national and international politics.

Economics has another advantage. Its assumptions are not difficult to identify. They are made explicit in introductory courses in economics. The task is simply to isolate them and to evaluate them. Some of this can be done even in the very brief discussions possible in a book of this sort.

Finally, selecting economics enables us to pick up a story begun in chapter 2 and discussed further in chapters 3 and 4, the story of Roger Schwartz.

For the institutional example, I choose higher education. Its full secularization in the United States has taken place in the past fifty years. The results have been mixed. It is worthwhile to consider them and to analyze the basic assumptions that they reflect and express.

I would not argue that the university is the most important institution in our society. I select it more because of my personal familiarity with it. Nevertheless, it *is* important. Much of the way our society thinks about many matters is affected by the way the university is organized. The university prepares the professionals who work in every field and thus forms their understanding of their roles. The research conducted in the university provides much of the information used in business and industry as well as by the military.

There is also a close connection between the assumptions of the university and economic theory. This makes it possible to tell a continuous story in what follows. The part of this story dealing with economics constitutes chapter 8. Chapter 9 continues with a discussion of the university.

DOING YOUR THEOLOGY

1. Do you agree that Christian faith has been pushed to the sidelines in the modern world? Do you see this as a gain or a loss, or some of both? Do you think it is time to critique the secular world from a Christian point of view? Why, or why not?

2. Identify the fields of study and the institutions with which you are most involved or most familiar. Have you thought of them as having assumptions that might be questioned? Have you criticized them? If so, have your criticisms been Christian ones?

3. Can you now identify assumptions that are operative in these fields and institutions that would be worth discussion? What are they? What would you say about them from a Christian point of view?

CHAPTER EIGHT

A Critique of Economics

1. Roger Schwartz and Pastor Philip Stewart

R oger Schwartz was serious about his faith. He made an appointment to see his pastor, the Reverend Philip Stewart, to talk with him about his sermon on economics. By the time of the appointment, he had calmed down considerably. He realized that Pastor Stewart knew little about the business world and spent much more time with the Bible.

"Reverend," Mr. Schwartz said, when the formalities were over, "I made this appointment because your sermon last Sunday bothered me. In fact it made me quite angry. You seemed to say that Christians should not seek to make a profit in their businesses, that they should be more concerned for what happens to their employees and competitors than to succeed themselves. But that would be a sure recipe for failure. If to be a Christian one had to adopt that ethics, then there is no way that a businessman can be a Christian."

"I do appreciate your telling me frankly how you reacted to my sermon, Roger. You took me seriously, maybe too seriously. I probably got carried away by my own rhetoric. Just last week I was counseling with a victim of sharp business practices who felt with good reason that her life had been ruined by them. According to her story, it would have taken so little consideration on the part of her boss to have saved the situation for her that I was really quite angry about his ruthlessness. I'm afraid that came out in what I said. I really doubt in that instance that it was good business practice."

"Then you don't really believe that it is wrong to pursue profits vigorously and single-mindedly as is required for success in business?" Roger Schwartz asked. "I learned in my courses in economics that if we all do that, even though some are hurt in the short run, the economy becomes more efficient, and the whole society benefits. I had some problem reconciling this apparent selfishness with what I had been taught by my parents and church school teachers, but I decided there was no other way to act than the one I was taught in business school. I suppose your sermon made me angry because it aroused all those painful feelings I thought I had laid to rest."

"This is a really tough question," Pastor Stewart replied. "I'm afraid I don't know what to think. Many years ago I was attracted to socialism because its idea that we should work for the benefit of society, rather than selfishly, seemed so much more Christian. But it did not take a lot of reading about socialist countries to persuade me that it didn't work.

"Even so, I'm not sure that capitalism is working very well either. I read about the conditions in factories built by U.S. capital on the Mexican side of the Rio Grande, and I am appalled. At the same time I read about the closing of factories in this country, and I think about what that does to thousands of families, and I am appalled by that, too. The businessmen are doing just what you affirm, seeking as much profit as possible, but I'm not sure that either the U.S. or Mexico is better off."

"The economists assure us," Roger Schwartz responded, "that investing in the most profitable way increases production, and that the increase of production means that there will be more goods for lower prices. Society *will* benefit, even if there is disruption of the lives of some people. The standard of living overall will rise."

"Maybe so," Pastor Stewart did not sound entirely convinced. "Economics is not my expertise. It is just that I see so many hurting people. And even though our Gross National Product has gone up a lot in the last twenty years, we seem as a people less able, or less willing, to respond to the hurt. We don't even have enough money to educate our children properly. Economists tell us we are a lot better off, and we do have more gadgets, but we also have a lot more hungry and homeless people, a lot more crime, more broken homes, and less hope. It seems to me that there is something wrong with the way economists measure 'progress.' "

"I worry about some of those things, too," Roger Schwartz admitted. "I don't feel good about the world we're leaving to my kids. I don't think it is the fault of us business people, but I'm not as confident as I once was that we are improving the situation for society as a whole. Something doesn't feel right."

"If you are serious about this, Roger, I would like to encourage you to get together with a few other Christians to study it. I can hardly imagine a more important question for Christians to work on. We preachers on the whole don't have much to contribute. Laypeople like you need to guide the church in its thinking. Still, I would like to be included in the group."

Roger Schwartz *was* serious, and with Pastor Stewart's help, he got the group together. The group included Peggy Ray, the businesswoman mentioned in chapter 2 and Margaret Williamson, a biologist who taught at a nearby university and was active in the Sierra Club. They agreed that they needed an economist, but there were none in the congregation. They invited Harvey Finkelstein, who taught historical economics at a nearby liberal arts college and was well known for his humanistic interests. Finding a time when all five were free was a bit complicated, but they finally met.

2. Anthropocentrism

Roger Schwartz opened the discussion by explaining again why he was so concerned. "It has never been easy for me to reconcile my Christian beliefs about unselfishness and generosity with the practices that seem essential to successful business. I have resolved the tension by trusting that economists are right that as we each act in terms of our self-interest, society as a whole benefits. The biblical writers, of course, could not have known that; so since they, too, wanted the well-being of society as a whole, I have found it right as a Christian to follow the rules of good business practice and to oppose governmental interference.

"Over the thirty years of my business practice, the economy in this country and elsewhere has grown a great deal—just as the economists hoped and predicted. But when I look around me and read the papers, I am not satisfied. Many of us have more goods, but poverty seems to have grown worse. Families are breaking up more and more. More people use drugs. There is more crime. Schools seem to be declining. What is wrong?

"Some economists tell us that what we need is more growth so that we will have the resources to deal with all these problems. For a long time I was convinced. Now I wonder. It seems that the problems are growing faster than the economic resources. And there is something about the moral climate that bothers me, too. People don't seem to be as concerned to solve the social problems as they once were. They seem more likely just to want to protect themselves from those problems, to make sure their own children don't suffer. Years ago I thought that we could behave according to self-interest in the market and then work for justice as Christians in other contexts. Now it seems that self-interest governs more and more of our lives. Maybe it is not so easy to divide our lives in that way.

"It is my hope that we can talk about economics very seriously in this group. I have thought of it as a science that is simply true. Now I wonder. Maybe it operates with a particular picture of the world that is not entirely accurate. Maybe the Christian faith has some wisdom that economists need to learn. For a long time Christians like me have simply accepted what scientists told them. Maybe we need to ask questions."

Margaret Williamson chimed in. "Before we begin asking questions about economic theory, there is another aspect of what is happening around us that is very important to me, and I think it should be important to everyone. As our economy grows, the ecology declines. Almost all the things we do to increase the size of the economy tend to exhaust our natural resources, pollute our environment, and destroy our wilderness. I'm a field ecologist, and it is a depressing vocation. Everywhere I go, I see the biosphere in decay."

Professor Finkelstein was growing a bit irritated. "There is no shortage of problems, to be sure. But this is partly because our expectations have grown even faster than our ability to fulfill them. If we take a long-term view, we can see what enormous progress we have made. Even many people we call poor in this country have luxuries that were not available to princes a hundred years ago. We are impatient for all to be rich. That will take a while. But we must not give up the system that has brought us all this progress just because it has not yet solved all the problems!"

"I do realize, Professor Finkelstein," said Pastor Stewart, "that we are impatient and that we take for granted an affluence that was very rare in the past. Indeed, it is very rare now in many parts of the world. And I realize that we express appreciation for what has been achieved less than we bemoan present suffering. But I am beginning to suspect that many of the problems we face now are not going to be solved if we continue in our present direction. They are not problems with which a growing economy helps us. They are instead by-products of growth or, more accurately, of the policies we adopt to stimulate growth.

"This is most apparent with regard to the ecological problems to which Margaret called our attention. Economic growth means using our resources faster and polluting the environment more. When people propose protecting the environment, economists often object that this will slow growth. Isn't there a real problem here?"

"Yes, there is," Professor Finkelstein answered. "Until recently resource economics and environmental economics hardly existed. There was some acknowledgment that what we call externalities, that is, costs and benefits to third parties, should be factored into prices, but few economists worked on this. Economics is in need of a good bit of fine-tuning to do its job properly. Like everybody else, we work on the problems that seem most important at the time, and until recently those did not include environmental ones.

"On the other hand, we must beware of those who have romantic views of nature and want to stop progress so as to preserve it just the way it is. Progress depends on reshaping our environment. We can preserve bits and pieces of the landscape. Economists can even give rational guidance in that process by determining how valuable the preservation of those bits and pieces is in comparison with other uses. They can survey the people who are affected and determine how much they would be willing to pay to preserve a certain bit of landscape. This is not as reliable a measure as what people actually do pay in the market, but it enables us to make rough and ready comparisons. The system that leads to progress is the one that allocates resources to their most valuable use. And the science of economics is designed to show how that is done—chiefly by allowing market forces to work, but also by valuing some goods that are not for sale on the market."

Margaret Williamson could not accept this. "I understand that one of the things our group wants to do is to identify assumptions underlying economic theory and practice. When we identify them, then we can discuss their merits. One assumption is very clear in what Professor Finkelstein has said, and I think he accurately reflects economic theory at its best.

"That assumption is that the real value of anything is what people are willing to pay for it. That is completely anthropocentric. It means that an ecosystem or a species that evolved over millions of years is worth nothing unless it is useful to human beings or unless some human beings just happen to want to preserve it. I can't accept that.

"In any case, people often don't know enough about the usefulness of things to put a proper price on them. Usually they begin to appreciate the real value of those things only after they have destroyed most of them. Wetland ecology happens to be my specialty. Until recently, hardly anyone appreciated the enormous services that wetlands provide for human beings—quite apart from the wonderful ecosystems they contain. Now that we have destroyed half our wetlands, we are beginning to realize what we are losing and the costs of providing substitutes. Even George Bush promised to put an end to the net loss of wetlands. Unfortunately, he fulfilled that promise by redefining wetlands so that more acres could be 'developed' or farmed. As long as economic considerations dominate, we will continue shortsighted policies."

"You are correct," Professor Finkelstein responded, "that economics is anthropocentric; that value means value for human beings is one of its assumptions. I cannot imagine how that assumption could be changed and there could still be any economic theory at all. It is certainly well to take that assumption into consideration. But isn't the only alternative just the sort of romantic naturalism that would block human progress? Isn't anthropocentrism the correct assumption to make? I am not a Christian, but isn't anthropocentrism an assumption made by Christians too? As an historian of economics, I suspect that anthropocentrism was an assumption that economics took over from its Christian context with very little reflection, just because it was rarely questioned.

"Your other point seems more important to me. We should value everything in terms of its actual economic services to human beings. We are often ignorant of many of these services. Until recently, economists tended to ignore them. That was a mistake. Some of us are now working hard to put dollar values on natural resources such as wetlands. It is partially our success in doing so that has led to changes in policy.

"I do not mean that we deserve all the credit. On the contrary, people like you called our attention to the economic value of wetlands. We need you to keep pushing us, since we as a community are more comfortable studying the market than pricing goods that cannot readily be bought and sold on the market."

Pastor Stewart was pleased that one of the assumptions of economic theory and practice had been identified so clearly. "You are probably correct, Professor Finkelstein, that the Christianity in the context of which economic theory arose was anthropocentric. It was, of course, also theocentric, but at least in the West, its belief in God as Creator did not lead it to value the rest of the creation for its own sake. It read the story of creation as subordinating everything else to human beings and especially to the human soul.

"But I was struck by your saying that you cannot imagine an economic theory that is not anthropocentric in this sense. I can certainly imagine Christian theology without that character. Indeed, most Christian thinkers today oppose anthropocentrism and place a positive value on the rest of creation. Rereading the creation story, they realize that God did not see that other creatures were good only in their usefulness to human beings.

They were good in themselves. God commanded Noah to save all the species, not just those of use to people.

"The World Council of Churches has committed itself to 'peace, justice, and the integrity of creation.' There are many views as to just what the 'integrity of creation' means, but almost all who discuss it agree that it is a rejection of thoroughgoing anthropocentrism. It seems that we have identified one point where contemporary Christian thinking is critical in an important assumption of economic theory."

3. Faith in Technology

Peggy Ray entered the discussion. "There is another feature of economic theory that bothers me. It is always people who are now alive who set values on things. Since most of us do not think very far into the future, we value things according to how they affect us now and in the short term. That allows us to use particular resources freely, even though they are likely to be exhausted, perhaps in fifty years. As long as they are plentiful now, the market prices them cheaply. Our descendants don't have a chance to protest."

"This is an objection that is often made to letting the market set prices," Professor Finkelstein replied. "But I do not think it is valid. It is true that at present the future shortage of oil does not affect its price. Some of the oil producers tried to jack up prices through artificial shortages, but fortunately OPEC did not succeed for long. It is far better to let the market do its work.

"In time, oil supplies will grow scarce. That time can be postponed by additional discoveries and technological advances, but it will come. As that time comes close, people will buy up oil in anticipation of rising prices, and this will speed up their rise. As prices rise, sources that are not now profitable to exploit will come back into operation. Users will find ways to use the oil more efficiently. And with technological advances, substitutes for oil will be found. Market forces will insure a smooth transition to a society based on other forms of energy. The anxiety now expressed by doomsayers is not justified."

"I don't agree with you," said Peggy Ray. "You may be right when you focus simply on oil supplies. Actually, the pressure to substitute does not await their scarcity, since their use is the major source of the threat of global warming, as well as smog and the dying of forests. The changes you say will come about through market forces are being brought about now in an effort to reduce pollution. These efforts would be aided if economists would help us price petroleum in terms of all its social costs.

"But my real concern is that economists seem to think in quite linear ways, as your example illustrates. You can speak of market forces solving the problem without considering the alternative sources of energy and the social and ecological costs involved in most of them. One move would be to nuclear energy, and there are certainly those who want that. But even if there were no other problems, that of disposing of nuclear wastes warns us that this is not a good solution. Coal would be a stopgap solution with horrendous ecological problems. Producing gasohol from agricultural products would help, but it would require vast acreage that will be increasingly needed by a growing population for the production of food. Solar energy is promising, but even proposals for solar energy production, when it is on a large scale, are problematic from an environmental point of view. It is not possible for benign forms of solar energy to meet our needs in the foreseeable future unless there are vast changes of other sorts in the way we produce food, house ourselves, and organize markets."

Professor Finkelstein was not impressed. "The fact that we cannot now know what technologies will be developed to meet our needs is not important. Technology has always developed as rapidly as it was needed in the past. Often it has been well ahead of the need. There is no reason to think that this will be different in the future. Our ability to control the natural world has grown by leaps and bounds. The rate of technological development accelerates. We have no reason to be pessimistic about the future."

"Thanks, Professor Finkelstein," said Peggy Ray, "you have made quite explicit another assumption of current economic theory. Let's call it faith in technology. It is because I don't share that faith that I am troubled about the future. I think we are moving into a new situation in which technology is more the problem than the solution. The chemical revolution released

117

thousands of artificial chemical compounds into the environment with unknown and often deleterious effects. The nuclear revolution produces substances that are extremely poisonous and will be so for tens of thousands of years. I confess that I expect the biotechnological revolution, driven by market forces, to produce a new set of critical problems. I am not saying that technological advance is all bad. But I am saying that faith that it will solve all our problems is misplaced. In fact, new technology often generates problems faster than it solves them."

Roger Schwartz spoke again. "Congratulations, Peggy. I think it is clear that you have identified a second assumption of contemporary economics, one that is just as crucial as anthropocentrism. Economists believe that market forces trigger human ingenuity so that solutions will be found to problems as they arise. If that is not true, or if, as you suggest, the solutions generate more problems than they solve, then economic theory needs to be significantly recast. Currently, its faith in technology allows it largely to ignore what is physically occurring on the surface of the earth. If it did not have this faith, it would have to examine the physical effects of economic activity much more carefully.

"The question for us now is whether Christians share this faith in technology. Or is this an assumption of which Christians are properly critical, as Peggy is? What do you think, Reverend Stewart?"

"I think those of us who are Christian need to address that question just as Peggy has. My sense is that Christianity in this case, too, gave some encouragement to faith in technology. Christians have celebrated human dominion over the earth in ways that freed them to reshape it to their ends. We have emphasized human freedom and ability as God's great gifts to us. We have also taught that God cares for us, and that because of the power of God, the future is ultimately secure. During the seventeenth and eighteenth centuries, the period we call the Enlightenment, this security, derived from God's providential care, became confidence that human ingenuity would bring about a better world. By emphasizing that God works through us, Christians often went along with this secularization of their hope. In these and other ways, Christians, and especially we Protestant Christians, have given a lot of support to faith in technology.

Probably most of us share it, or at least have shared it until quite recently.

"But, of course, this is a one-sided reading of Christian teaching. Christians have emphasized human finitude and sinfulness. We know that we are not to be trusted with great power. Even with the best of intentions, we are likely to misuse it because of ignorance. And in fact we are quite suspicious of our own intentions. We know that we are able to pretend to others, and even to ourselves, that our intentions are better than they really are. When we turn this power over to market forces based on short-term self-interest, we have little reason to expect that it will be used wisely and well.

"Overall, therefore, I do not think that the Christian faith encourages us to have faith in technology. It does not oppose technology, but it suggests that technological developments, like political power, should be subordinated to checks and balances that prevent them from being controlled simply by market forces. Without such checks they are likely to become demonic. Instead of being used for the good of society, they blindly reshape society. No, we cannot place our faith in technology."

The members of the congregation agreed; there was a second assumption of contemporary economics of which the Christians felt they should be critical.

4. Economic Growth as Overarching Goal

Roger Schwartz turned the discussion back to his original concerns. "We've focused on the ecological and environmental questions Margaret raised rather than on the social ones of which I spoke initially. I expressed my concern that our social problems are growing faster than our ability to deal with them. Pastor Stewart raised the question whether our economic growth, or rather the policies that support it, intensify these problems. If so, then trying to grow fast enough to gain the resources to solve them will not work. What do you think, Professor Finkelstein?"

"As with so many such topics, matters are far from simple," Professor Finkelstein began. "It is true that some costs are involved in the industrialization that is required for growth. Chiefly this is because industrialization requires urbanization, and cities require complex infrastructures. It also seems that, on the whole, urban life may be less healthy than rural life, and that crime rates are likely to be higher in the city. The Gross National Product can be legitimately criticized for not taking some of these costs of growth into consideration. But doing so would have only a slight effect on the calculation of the rate of economic growth.

"However, you are listing all kinds of problems, such as the decline in the quality of education, that are surely not the result of economic growth! On the contrary, economic growth made it possible greatly to increase the resources at the disposal of public education—and private education, too, for that matter. Teachers are better paid, even in comparison with other professions, than they were twenty years ago, and physical resources are better. If education is not better, that is because of noneconomic changes. The economy has performed as it should on this front."

"You are right," Roger Schwartz replied, "that education is better funded now than it was in the past. Teachers are better paid. And you are right that the reasons for decline are social rather than economic. Adolescent culture is less influenced by adult culture than in the past, and it is far more violent. Parental participation in the education of children has declined in many communities, partly because of the breakdown of the family generally. More children are involved with alcohol and other drugs. These are not directly economic matters.

"But I am wondering whether, indirectly, they are not related to economic changes. Economic theory favors the substitution of capital for labor in order to improve productivity. The effect of this in the years after World War II was greatly to increase the productivity of agricultural labor. But the flip side of that was a large movement of population from the stable community life in the countryside to big cities. These cities were not in position to absorb all these people into well-paying productive jobs. Many of them swelled the welfare roles and contributed to the ghetto culture that often lacks a vision of a hopeful future.

"More recently the flow of capital to places where it could be more profitably invested has led to hundreds of factory closings in what is called the rustbelt. Long-established and prosperous industrial communities have been destroyed. Workers have followed capital to the South where unions are weaker and wages have been lower. It takes a while to reestablish stable communities. Extended families, and even nuclear families, are broken up by these moves. Children are more subject to peer pressure when they do not grow up in stable communities.

"The problem is still more critical when the factories move overseas or across the Rio Grande. Workers cannot follow them there. They must be retrained. But rarely are other jobs available at the same wage level. Real wages overall are in decline. That is demoralizing. The demoralization of parents takes its toll on children.

"It is for reasons such as this that I am coming to think that Reverend Stewart's suggestion is correct. Depopulation of the countryside with its destruction of thousands of small towns and rapid movement of capital investment, much of it out of the country, contribute to a social decline that changes the climate of our public schools for the worse. Perhaps very large investments that would greatly reduce the student-teacher ratio could turn things around, but there are many other increasing demands on public funds to meet the growing social needs. There is no prospect of a vast infusion of new funds into public education."

"I am sure that you greatly overstate the role of economic developments in shaping adolescent culture," replied Professor Finkelstein, "but even if you are correct, I cannot see that we have any alternative. Increased productivity is essential for growth. That requires repeated dislocation of labor in the sense that labor must go where capital investments are most productive. To try to block this movement of capital can only lead to economic stagnation.

"The recession we have recently experienced, which has made it more difficult to address our social and ecological needs, is nothing in comparison with what would happen if we tried to keep capital tied up in unproductive enterprises. American capital cannot compete with that in other countries if it is always bound to high labor and environmental costs. Moving into a truly global economy is a great challenge, and it will entail some sacrifices. But it is the only way to continue the growth on which a healthy economy depends. Without that growth there will be massive unemployment, and the demoralization of American workers will become much worse, together with the social problems you identify. And there will be fewer and fewer resources with which to respond."

"I think I detect another assumption," said Roger Schwartz. "It is that economic growth is and should be the central aim of economic policy. Am I correct?"

"Yes," replied Finkelstein, "there is no alternative. At whatever social and environmental cost, we *must* grow. Without growth, the social and environmental problems cannot even be addressed. The idea of a no-growth economy simply makes no sense."

"Is that the sort of scientific truth," Roger Schwartz wondered out loud, "that Christians must simply accept? Or if we put our minds to it, is it possible that we can envision an economy that meets human needs without necessarily growing? If the costs of growth both to the environment and to society are so high, it does seem that we Christians have reason to make the try. Since there have been societies in the past whose economies were not based on growth, it does not seem that this assumption is beyond question."

"You Christians are a strange lot," commented Professor Finkelstein. "We economists are building on a two hundred year development of a complex science that has been enormously successful. You seem to be proposing to build a new economic theory and a new economic system out of whole cloth on the basis of untried and untested assumptions. Do you think this is realistic?"

"No!" Pastor Stewart laughed. "It is certainly not realistic. But I wonder whether it is realistic to continue on the road we are now traveling. The prospects seem awfully bleak to me. And your replies to our questions have not been reassuring. We must continue to grow, you say, even if the process of growth worsens our situation. Surely we can do better than that! Even if we have no sensible proposals to make, we are at least answering the theological question with which we began. Must we as Christians accept the whole of economic theory as objectively true and replace our biblical and traditional teachings about human beings and human relations with those assumptions that are employed in economic theory? We have said, 'No, we have the right to be critical of some of them. And we have the right to make some suggestions about the economic order based on different and more Christian assumptions.' "

5. Homo Economicus and Market Size

"There is another assumption," Professor Finkelstein commented, "that I was expecting you to question. Economic theory operates with a particular idea about human nature. This is called *Homo economicus. Homo economicus* is understood to be a rational individual, that is, one who seeks to get as many goods as possible and to work as little as possible. Of course, no one thinks that this economic model of the human being is adequate for all purposes, but it has been remarkably adequate for the analysis of economic activity, and economists are now demonstrating that it is useful in other fields as well. Still outsiders often challenge and even ridicule it. Are you accepting it?"

Roger Schwartz smiled. "It is just this aspect of economic theory that first troubled me. Indeed, I went to see Reverend Stewart because he objected to us businessmen operating in terms of that model, seeking, that is, to maximize profits even when people are hurt in the process. I was sure there was no alternative except to get out of business. I still suspect that is true.

"But I am beginning to change my mind on one point. In the past I have been opposed to government regulations in general on the ground that they inhibit the market and thus slow growth. I think the commitment to growth comes out of this model of the human being. All that is important for this human being is to get as many goods as possible for as little work as possible. Therefore, increasing production with reduced labor is the goal, and that means improved productivity and growth.

"Maybe we should consider other human needs besides leisure and consumption. For example, people care about their relations to others. Human community is important to them. They like to be contributors to their community and feel supported by it. They also care about the conditions under which they work and about being treated with respect. Perhaps we could redefine the goal of the economy in terms of a healthy community within which all people have the opportunity to do enjoyable work and to meet their real economic needs.

123

"When the only goals are productivity and growth, the market is the right instrument. The less it is controlled, the better. But if the real goals of economic life are different, then these goals should be set by society, and rules for market activity should channel that activity accordingly.

"I still think that *Homo economicus* describes us quite accurately as far as our market activity is concerned. If my competitor takes actions that are destructive of community, I must do so also, or else lose out. But if we can jointly see to it that such actions are ruled out by law, then we can compete without acting in those ways. As a Christian I should, and now I will, rejoice in government regulations that have the effect of enabling me to act toward others in less ruthless ways, although that doesn't mean that I will enjoy dealing with another bunch of regulatory agencies!"

Peggy Ray was pleased with Roger Schwartz's comments. The necessity for ruthlessness that is built into market competition had always been deeply repugnant to her. "There is still a problem in what you propose, Roger. If the economy operated primarily within national boundaries, the national government could restrict the actions of all businesses, making it harder for them to close factories and relocate where wages are lower, for example. But the market today is international, even global. If our government restricted us further, our competitiveness with foreign producers would erode even more. Frankly, we would be put out of business altogether.

"I think there is a solution, but it would require a fundamental redirection of both thought and practice. It has been axiomatic that the larger the market, the better. This allows for increased specialization and economies of scale. It also allows for increased capital mobility, that is, the investment of capital where it is most productive and profitable. All that makes sense when growth is the primary goal.

"But if we care more about meeting a wider range of human needs in community, then none of it makes sense! We need smaller markets governed by the people they serve. At their largest they should be national markets, but I think, in fact, local and regional markets would work better for these purposes."

"Now you really are going off the deep end," Professor

Finkelstein exploded. "I take it you want to renew protectionisms of all sorts and even abolish the freedom of interstate commerce. Back to the Middle Ages or worse!

"And have you considered what this would mean for Third World countries whose only hope for escaping from miserable poverty is to export more to us? Renewed isolationism on our part would plunge the whole global system into chaos. The depression that would result would be far worse than that of the thirties. As Christians, how can you even contemplate such a move?"

Peggy Ray was taken aback by the professor's vehemence. "You may be right, of course. I have hardly thought these matters through. And I know that any change in direction should be made gradually with plenty of warning.

"But I wonder whether drawing the Third World into the global trading system has really helped most of the Third World peoples. It pushes them to specialize in a few products, often agricultural ones. To achieve that, often the peasant land is expropriated and turned over to agribusiness. Millions of people, and indeed whole nations, that were once able to feed and clothe themselves, now depend on imports whose prices they can hardly influence.

"For the sake of competing more successfully in this global market, many Third World countries are being forced to 'restructure' their economies. That means greatly reduced support for their poor, who are already very poor. And I am not sure that when factories are built in those countries just to produce goods for export, they benefit the people there very much. If the world decided to move in the direction I am proposing, many of those factories could be regeared to produce for import-substitution purposes rather than for export. And agricultural land could again be used to feed those who live upon it. I believe world hunger would decline."

"Peggy may not be right in all her details," Roger Schwartz chimed in, "but her general point is convincing. It is becoming clearer to me how central has been the commitment to growth in determining the whole direction of economic thinking, and how closely that has been bound up with the model of *Homo economicus*. It would be better to understand the goals of human life served by the economy in terms of a different model of the human being, such as 'person-in-community.'

"We can still recognize that buying and selling goods in the market is well-interpreted by the classical *Homo economicus*. Being persons-in-community does not keep us from bargain hunting or trying to make a profit on our sales. In this narrow sphere, we do try to sell as high as we can and buy as cheaply as possible, and this 'selfishness' generally leads to efficiency in the allocation of resources.

"But the enlarging on the market for the sake of encouraging growth works against human community. It might take a lot of experimenting to find the size of market in various places that would allow for a sufficient supply of goods and services to meet the needs of people, with sufficient competition to encourage efficiency, and yet would not support the movement of capital investment from one part of the market to another. I'm convinced that if economists accepted this changed goal, they could quickly help in answering questions of this sort.

"Another assumption of economics seems to be that its model of the human being as an individual who seeks to acquire as much as possible with as little labor as possible is adequate for developing economic theory. It is clear that we think it has a more limited usefulness. I also think we believe this criticism is an appropriate one for Christians to make."

Pastor Stewart sensed that they were all tired and that continuing the discussion would not be very fruitful. He also sensed that it had been hard on their special guest, Professor Finkelstein. "We all want to thank you, Professor Finkelstein, for putting up with us in this way. Without your patient help, we wouldn't have gotten anywhere. I know you do not agree with many of our ideas, but for us it has been very valuable. We are truly in your debt."

"Thanks," replied Professor Finkelstein. "This has all seemed strange to me. My colleagues think I'm a bit radical myself, but I've never even been exposed to anything like this before. I can't agree with much that you are saying, but you have forced me to realize how little we economists reflect about our own assumptions. We are so sure that we are on the right track that we pay very little attention to most criticisms by outsiders and even to the occasional criticism from within. As social and environmental problems get worse, I suspect that the kinds of criticisms you are raising will cease to sound altogether crazy. They may even stimulate some real debate among economists. You've given me a chance to get a head start in reflecting about these issues. So I owe you a debt as well."

Doing Your Theology

1. Do you agree that Christians should "counterattack" the world in the sense of critically examining the assumptions of economics and other disciplines and proposing alternatives? Or should Christians leave all fields of thought to the specialists? Is there a third possibility? Explain your preference theologically.
2. Evaluate one or more of the criticisms directed against orthodox economics offered in this chapter. Are your evaluations theological? If so, how?
3. Does the general direction for the economy suggested by this discussion make sense to you as a Christian? Or does today's dominant direction seem better? Explain your answer theologically.

CHAPTER NINE

A Critique of the University

1. Criticizing Assumptions

*M*argaret Williamson had been rather quiet after her first intervention, but she was staying very much with the discussion. Like many ecologists, she had resented the economists for some time. Here was a group of Christians who did not just resent and complain, but also analyzed. She was glad that the problem with economics was not only the anthropocentrism that had upset her so much so long. That meant that there could be a more concerted opposition and maybe the emergence of real alternatives.

But what struck her even more forcefully was that conversations like this seemed never to take place in academia. She had been teaching in universities for more than twenty years, and she had never heard a sustained analysis of the assumptions underlying any academic discipline! Why was that?

The university often talked of itself as a place of unfettered inquiry. As she realized how much of that "unfettered " inquiry was governed by the military-industrial complex, she had often spoken cynically about it. But what she saw now was something still more fundamental. Even in that part of the life of academia not governed by outside financial pressures, even when the inquiry was in some sense free, it never seemed to be directed toward these fundamental questions.

Even though she thought she had seen everything and was impervious to being shocked again, the realization that the most basic questions were not asked within the university did shock her. She had known that most university research served the rich and the powerful. Now she saw that the university did not encourage serious thinking. She could not explain this just in terms of the power of money to direct attention. Professors in the various departments really did have considerable freedom with respect to what they taught. Why did they not analyze the assumptions of their own disciplines, or even of one another's disciplines? She was genuinely perplexed as well as saddened.

If this kind of inquiry doesn't go on in the university, perhaps the church is the place, she decided. She would see if Pastor Stewart would help her get a group together to talk about the university. Surely that was an important topic, too.

Stewart was a bit startled by this idea. Whereas he had been disturbed by economic teaching and practice for a long time, he had taken it for granted that universities were basically on the side of the angels. They sought truth, and they imparted information and wisdom. But then, again, economics was a very prestigious discipline within the university. And if economists never discussed the assumptions of economics in a critical way, perhaps there was something missing in the ethos of the university that should be critically examined.

The question, then, was whom to invite. They decided to ask Roger Schwartz to come to this discussion; they were impressed by his insights. Then there was Harry Baskin, a philosopher at the same university as Dr. Williamson, who attended the church and might be interested. At first, they could not think of anyone who had studied the university itself, but Dr. Williamson remembered reading about a study done in the department of education about some facet of higher education. She had not paid much attention at the time, but she thought the writer was now an associate dean of the college. Her name was Beth Turner, and she seemed a good bet as a source of information and maybe of ideas as well.

All the invitees accepted, and eventually a time and a place were agreed on and the group gathered. Margaret initiated the discussion. She told Dr. Baskin and Dean Turner about the previous meeting with Professor Finkelstein. "Afterward, when I reflected on that meeting, I was startled to realize that the questions we were raising are not discussed in departments of economics. The whole discipline is based on assumptions that seemed quite shaky to us, and the course of events in the public world is shaped by the judgments that follow from those assumptions. I suppose that most people think economists have selected their assumptions carefully and critically, so that their 'science' is reliable. Perhaps they suppose that in the university we are all under pressure to scrutinize our assumptions. But I realized that I had never encountered any such scrutiny in my own department, and I had never heard of it in other departments. That made me think that there is something wrong with the university as a whole. I hope I'm wrong, and I'll be glad if you can show me that I'm wrong."

2. The Academic Disciplines

Dean Turner was the first to speak. "You invited me primarily because you knew that I had done some research on universities. My study was a sociological one about the structure of power in universities. I was particularly interested in the relative power of faculties and administrators and the roles played by deans. As you can see, I've ended up as one of the latter! I'm not sure that what I learned from that study will be of much help here.

"But I was struck by one thing that may be relevant. Considering the importance of the university as an institution, and considering how many sociologists are at work in that institution, it is noteworthy that there is very, very little sociological study of the university.

"I'm sure that is not accidental. Actually, I found a lot of resistance to my own study. It seemed that I was violating an unspoken taboo. Professors like to objectify everybody else in their studies, but the idea of being objectified themselves does not sit well with them. They don't want their disciplines or their institution treated that way.

"Of course, quite a few books have been written about universities, their purposes and their failures. But they generally paint with a rather broad brush. Perhaps the most interesting discussion recently has been about curriculum, especially about the idea that there is a canon. Some say that there is a set of books that are crucial to the education of all. Others reply that every definition of a canon is a way of making one strand within our culture normative and silencing competing voices. That debate certainly brings out some basic assumptions. But I am not aware that much has been written on the assumptions that govern the several disciplines."

Roger Schwartz was not quite clear about what Dr. Williamson was after. "I certainly understood at that other meeting that we were looking for the assumption of economics. That made a lot of sense to me, and I suppose something like that might be done in the other social sciences. But surely the natural sciences are not based on doubtful assumptions in that same way. For example, would a critique of assumptions make any sense in biology?"

"I've been thinking about that a lot recently," Dr. Williamson replied. "And my answer is yes. Probably I see that more easily than most biologists because I am a field ecologist, and we tend to look at things quite differently from the way biologists who work mainly in laboratories see them. Nowadays even many ecologists work more with computer models than actually in the field.

"Those of us who do still work in the field think that our colleagues miss something. They treat animals and plants and even ecosystems as if they were complex machines. Indeed, that is the assumption that I would most want to emphasize and criticize in biology. Biologists study organisms, but overwhelmingly they study those aspects of organisms that can be modeled as machines.

"Obviously, the mechanical model brings out a lot of features of organisms. This is very similar to the point we discussed at the other meeting, that the economists' model of human beings accurately reflects much about human behavior, especially in the market. But we agreed that using only that model misleads economists. The same thing is true with biologists—they miss some features of what they are studying.

"When you live with animals in the wild, you discover that they are individuals with temperamental differences. You know that they have a subjective life, just as you do, and that the effort to explain animal behavior apart from that individuality and subjectivity can only go so far. At a very fundamental level, it is just wrong; yet the orthodoxy of the discipline of biology is committed to that error.

"Let me give you one more example of the difference the basic model makes. With the mechanistic model, one assumes that one can study the parts of an organism and can build up an explanation of the whole out of this study. With an organismic model, one affirms that the behavior of the part is affected by its place in the whole and cannot be adequately understood when, in the laboratory, it is removed from the organism. Similarly, when an individual animal is removed from its normal context in the wild, its behavior and even its body chemistry change. This has been demonstrated again and again. But the basic model continues to ignore these characteristic features of organisms."

"Thanks," said Mr. Schwartz. "I think I see better now why you think this failure to criticize assumptions is a general one in the university. And if that is true, you are right to be concerned about the ethos of the university that does not encourage such self-criticism."

It was Dr. Baskin's turn: "I've been trying to decide whether we philosophers discuss our assumptions any more critically than do others. It is a strange question in a way. What is philosophy if it is not self-conscious critical inquiry?

"On the other hand, I guess the absence of effective criticism of the assumptions of the other disciplines follows from the abandonment of that task by philosophy. Philosophy used to be an overarching reflection on first principles, and that meant on the assumptions that underlie research in every field. Classical philosophers also tried to synthesize the findings in various fields into a unified vision. Only a few philosophers pursue such tasks today, and they are looked on a bit askance by the rest of us. Those tasks seem to be too ambitious or too pretentious.

"Philosophers do tend to discuss their individual assumptions. That may be a distinction between them and most other academicians. Yet, I suspect that you could make a case that we are not really very reflective about the assumptions of our discipline as a whole. We don't talk much about what counts as philosophy in general.

"If, for example, one studied the assumptions of biology and criticized them, would that be philosophy? Well, it could be. It would depend, probably, on the style in which the criticism was carried out, the positions to which reference was made, and, more than anything else, on whether the person who did the analysis was an accepted member of the philosophical community.

"It would be hard philosophically to justify the ways in which philosophers would decide this question. The boundaries of the academic discipline of philosophy are determined more by sociological considerations than by truly philosophical ones. Philosophers constitute a guild whose boundaries are somewhat fluid, but the criteria of membership are related more to socialization than to a clear definition of what constitutes philosophy. I doubt that the guild would appreciate the way I am describing it."

"Are you saying," Pastor Stewart asked, "that when philosophers gave up the task of examining basic assumptions across the board, no one else took it up? It sounds as though that may be the explanation of the extraordinary phenomenon of inattention to assumptions that has startled us so. The other disciplines left the task to philosophy, and philosophy decided not to continue with it. The consequences do seem to be serious!"

"There are times in the history of individual disciplines," Dean Turner commented, "when some of their assumptions are debated. New schools arise and contest the field. Behaviorism and cognitive psychology make quite different assumptions, and their advocates have argued about them. Even then, I'm sure, there were shared assumptions that went unnoticed. Another question is over how the issues are settled. My own bias, as you have guessed, is to look for a power struggle more than at the objective strength of the arguments put forth by the competing parties, but I'm sure that the latter plays some role. Then there is a more subtle factor of something like 'atmosphere.' Certain styles of inquiry are 'in' and others are 'out' at any given time. And especially for younger faculty, it is very important to be 'in.' "

"All of this would just be very interesting," said Dr. Williamson, "if so much were not at stake. That was most apparent in economics. But it is true to a lesser extent even in biology. The mechanistic mind-set supports the movement of much of our energy into biotechnology. I'm not totally opposed to biotechnology, but I am sure that humanity as a whole has a greater need to understand the natural world than to change it! One reason for the dominance of biotechnology is that the market is hungry for profits. But another reason is that the unexamined assumptions that control most biological research direct attention and enthusiasm to mastery and control.

"For the most part, it seems to me, the directions taken in the university are governed by two things. One is very obvious: the source of funding. Projects that lead to military advantage or profit for large businesses will obviously have high priority because they will be paid for. The second is the internal development of individual disciplines. That is the truly 'academic' side of the university, and we pride ourselves on this pure quest of knowledge. But when it is shaped by unexamined assumptions, it may not be so pure after all.

"One of the assumptions seems to be that research should be directed to the frontier of the discipline rather than by the needs of the world. That troubles me deeply as the world's needs become so very critical. Of course, there are some exceptions. But I fear that the word *academic* has come by its connotation of practical irrelevance honestly and fairly. It seems that the university attracts a large share of talent, provides time for thought and study, and then directs that thought and study away from the topics that so badly need illumination."

Roger Schwartz continued to be somewhat surprised by the harshness with which the academicians were criticizing themselves. "We outsiders often make jokes about the extreme specialization in the university," he said. "You seem to agree with that criticism. I gather that once you operate within an academic discipline or subdiscipline, your activities are pretty well channeled. You just deal with the problems that lie in that channel, whether or not they are of much use to the rest of the world."

3. The Assumptions of the University

Philip Stewart had been uncharacteristically silent, but he had been busy making notes. "I've heard a lot of criticism of what goes on in the university, and maybe that is all we want to do. But at the other meeting we found it fruitful to identify particular assumptions underlying economic theory. I've been trying to formulate some assumptions that seem to underlie the practice of the university. Of course, some of that practice is just a matter of economic survival. I suppose one assumption is that it is desirable to survive, but I'm not featuring that.

"The assumption that has stood out to me is that the university as a whole has no social purpose that guides the study and research of its parts. A second assumption is that knowledge can be divided among academic disciplines and that this is, indeed, the best way to pursue it. A third assumption is that these academic disciplines are mutually autonomous and define themselves and their own roles. A fourth assumption is that there is no need to examine either these assumptions of the university as a whole or whatever assumptions have managed to get themselves entrenched in the individual disciplines. How am I doing?"

"You are doing great," Dr. Baskin assured him. "If I didn't hear you preach every Sunday, I would think you were a philosopher! You said that at your other meeting you kept asking whether the assumptions you uncovered were acceptable to Christians. My immediate reaction is that none of them are. First, as Margaret has said, we live in a time of global crisis. A great institution such as the university should order its life so as to help humanity get through this. It needs a social purpose that would guide study and research in its parts.

"Second, if it had such a purpose, I doubt that it would organize itself along disciplinary lines. When it has been pushed to do something relevant, it has created special centers for such things as African-American studies, peace studies, and women's studies. On the whole, these have just been tolerated by the disciplinary departments and have tended to wither in the university atmosphere, but they could become models of a quite different organization. In that context, the academic disciplines would be related to each other through these centers, and ideally they would also recognize their capacity for mutual criticism and mutual support in other ways as well. The world they are studying is God's creation, and it is not divided into unrelated aspects.

"Finally, all disciplines, in order to qualify themselves as belonging to a community of responsible inquiry, would have to

135

clarify and defend their assumptions and change them when the defense is not convincing. My own discipline could again play a significant role in helping the other disciplines to do this. And some structure could be established to keep studying the university itself!"

4. Conclusions and Recommendations

This whole book has been about laypeople's taking responsibility for their own theology. The first six chapters dealt with theological issues in which professional Christian theologians also should be engaged. The argument was that theology should not be left to the theologians, that each of us must do his or her own believing, that the church will not regain vitality until many of us become reflective believers, clear about what we believe and why we believe it. For the sake of the church, that kind of lay theology is of the greatest importance.

But for the sake of the world, something else is needed. The West has been engaged in a protracted experiment in the secularization of its thought and of its institutions. This secularization has led to fragmentation. Questions of value have been pushed to the edges. The goals of society are little considered. We have a growing loss of direction and hence of meaning. The reasons for caring for one another, and especially for the poor and weak, are poorly articulated. Self-interest is more and more clearly shown to be an inadequate motive for action.

Christians often complain about the decline of society along these lines. But complaint and moral denunciation do not take us far. Unless our world makes sense to us and appropriate values are inherent in our major institutions, we will be in more and more trouble as time passes.

The church as an institution could do more than it does to respond to these problems, but its capacity is severely limited. The most important tasks are left to individual Christians and groups who see ways that their faith is significant and relevant. It is lay Christians especially who can make the difference. They are working in all the fields of inquiry and all the great institutions of our society. If they are challenged to think as Christians about these fields of inquiry and about these institutions, and if they can learn to do so effectively, Christian wisdom can begin to heal a sick society.

You are one of those lay Christians. Your place and role are not identical to anyone else's. Therefore, what you are called to do is not the same as what anyone else is called to do. I cannot pronounce on that, but I am convinced that the effort individually and in groups to think about the assumptions that shape our secular thought and society is urgent. We can all share in that. And when we do so, it may be easier than we suppose to bring our Christian faith to bear on crucial matters.

The stories in chapters 7 and 8 are told to encourage you in this enterprise. They reflect, of course, my judgment as to what assumptions underlie economics as a discipline and the university as an institution. They also reflect my views as to how Christians should appraise these assumptions. You may not agree with any of this. If the expression of my views leads you to clarify your own and to justify them as Christian, then my efforts will be well rewarded.

Becoming better theologians does not ensure that we will agree with one another. We have already noted that the results may be to make our differences sharper. At one level, that is regrettable. But a church engaged in serious debate over matters of great importance will be far healthier than the present one. And the world will benefit from a critical examination of its secular assumptions even if all Christians do not agree on the analysis and prescription.

Christians cannot afford a continued shrinking of the sphere within which we think *as Christians*. The world cannot afford to lose the benefit of Christian vision and wisdom. For the sake of both church and world, we all need to become better theologians.

DOING YOUR THEOLOGY

1. Academic disciplines other than economics are discussed briefly in this chapter. Have you any judgments about the assumptions that shape the work in these or still other disciplines? How do you evaluate the assumptions you

have identified? Do you understand your evaluation to be a Christian one? Explain.

2. Do you agree that the organization of the university shows a lack of any unifying purpose? Is this objectionable? If so, what purpose(s) should this institution serve?

3. If different disciplines operate from different assumptions, and if these are not compatible with one another, what does this imply about the nature of thought and of reality? Are these implications acceptable from a Christian point of view? Is any alternative possible?

An Afterword
on Church Theology

*T*heology plays many roles and takes on many legitimate forms. This book has been about one of those: that of the individual believer achieving explicit faith and developing it. Without that kind of theology becoming widespread in the oldline churches, these churches are doomed to continuing decline. No other type of theology will take its place.

More incidentally, the book has also talked about professional theology, which is, today, academic theology. It has discussed this theology only as it can serve personal theology. In fact, this theology has other roles to play in the public world, in the university, and in the institutional church, and all this deserves a discussion it has not received in this book.

But I have said almost nothing about church theology. That, too, means many things. Here I am speaking of the need of the church to express its shared convictions as a basis for common worship and common action in the world. This is required in local congregations, in denominations, and in ecumenical life. It requires thought, too, but this kind of thinking is different. To work that out responsibly is as large a task as the one to which this book is directed. Individual Christians need to appreciate that task and support it—in its difference.

There is a tension between the two kinds of theology. In the discussion of personal theology, I have stressed the need for total personal integrity. Our real, life-determining beliefs matter here.

I have contrasted these with the beliefs that many of us think we are *supposed* to hold. I have repeatedly indicated that focusing on the latter leads to inauthenticity. But the idea that we are supposed to hold these beliefs often arises because they are part of official church teaching, perhaps of ancient creeds. Thus the development of authentic, explicit faith and personal theology seems to involve the downgrading of church teaching!

There are several strategies of response to this problem. One is to reject all creeds. This has most often been a reaction to the divisiveness of doctrine. But it can also express the desire to give complete freedom for persons to think honestly for themselves.

Unfortunately, it has not worked well. Creedless churches turn out to be divisive, too, and even tend to be divided over beliefs. Often they develop unexpressed orthodoxies that are more restrictive than the creeds they replace. Or else they become radically nontheological, implying that their members' beliefs make little difference. This is not an argument for creeds, only that what appears to be the best and most straightforward solution does not solve the problem.

A second strategy is to develop detailed confessions. The fact that these succeed one another at intervals makes it clear that there is no pretense of having captured the truth in an immutable form. The authentic thinking of individual Christians can contribute to each new statement, even though the statement must express a consensus rather than the most distinctive features of the thought of individuals.

This is the approach of the Presbyterians, and it works well. It expresses the fact that theology plays a central role in their tradition, and it helps to keep theology alive as a vital force. It shows effectively that Christians have beliefs about many matters and that these are important.

It also has its problematic side. By spelling out so many supposedly shared convictions of its members, it goes rather far in telling them what they are *supposed* to think. Except for those few who are consciously involved in seeking change, working for new formulations in future confessions, this can have the inhibiting effect noted in this book. It can lead to the inauthentic theology of formal agreement with the teaching of the church while actually operating out of different convictions.

③ A third strategy is to seek to formulate a minimum statement. We may think of this as a statement of the shared beliefs of a particular community in which diversity is acknowledged and affirmed. This minimizes the tension between the authentic beliefs of free-thinking contemporary Christians, on the one side, and the official statement of what they are supposed to believe, on the other.

For example, the confession of the United Church of Christ is formulated in a way that few members of that community are likely to find offensive. It uses contemporary language to expresses what may be a consensus of most members. This largely solves the problem of inauthenticity generated by thinking one is supposed to believe some things that are not really part of one's basic belief system. But it does not go far in stimulating theological reflection on the part of its members.

④ A fourth strategy is that of The United Methodist Church. It inherited Articles of Religion from the Church of England, expressive of the Protestant self-definition against Rome at the time of the English Reformation. John Wesley abridged them but did not remove their anti-Catholic polemic. Obviously, they are not written in the language of today and are not expressive of the central convictions of most contemporary Methodists. Yet the Church is not free to reject them. Accordingly, it has located them in their historical context and described their present use and role. It has specifically rejected their anti-Catholic implications as well.

Instead of formulating a new statement of faith, this denomination has carried forward this style of describing its theological situation historically. This description includes an account of its special emphases as well as its continuity with the ecumenical church and its desire to remain a part of that. Instead of stating what its members should do or should believe, it discusses how they should do their theological thinking. In this connection, it highlights the quadrilateral, discussed in chapter 4.

This strategy reduces still further the tendency for church members to build an inauthentic theology on what they are supposed to think. Ideally it encourages just that authentic thinking for the sake of which I wrote this book. Unfortunately, it has not yet succeeded in this respect. Lay United Methodists have not actually been encouraged to think. Too often, they take their freedom to think freely as the freedom not to think at all. One problem, I am convinced, is that Christians need not only the space to think authentically, but also active guidance and help in the process of doing so. The Church has not offered this. This book seeks to help fill this need.

Denominations are relatively homogeneous communities of Christians, so they can work on the task of denominational theology in varied ways. As long as the way chosen fits the denominational culture, it is good theology. Working on denominational theology is quite different from the theological work this book is dedicated to promoting, but in all the instances listed, it is intended to allow for this more personal theology, if not actively to promote it. All of these programs are valid theological tasks to which those of us in quest of individual authenticity should give full support.

Furthermore, individual Christians, as they try to think authentically for themselves, can greatly profit from the work that is done by denominational leaders. Sometimes they can find in denominational statements solutions to problems that have perplexed them or introductions to issues of which they have not earlier been aware. Sometimes they can also contribute to the formulations that take on official status in their denominations.

All the denominations mentioned seek to display their unity with one another and with other Christian churches throughout the world. None of their strategies for denominational theology can be extended to ecumenical theology. All seek to speak in the real language of their own time, but this presupposes a measure of cultural homogeneity, and this presupposition cannot be extended to the worldwide church. Convincing and appropriate language in one culture sounds alien to persons in other cultures. Denominational theology developed in one culture often bypasses much of the traditional language of the church in those other cultures. When churches with widely varied histories come together, the basis of unity must be sought in what they have in common, and that usually means in the Christian thought of the period to which they all look back, the early church and, of course, the Bible.

But this creates problems. For ecumenical purposes, we stress our continuity with that shared history. For purposes of authentic Christian thinking today, we emphasize that the authority of what was done and said in those days interacts with the authority of much that has been learned since, both within and without the Christian community. This can lead to severe criticism of much that was done and said in the early period. For example, feminists have shown how pervasive and profound was the influence of patriarchy on the patterns of life and thought of the patristic church. How, then, can the uncriticized beliefs of that church be the basis of our unity?

The answer to that question requires thought, and much excellent thinking has taken place in the World Council of Churches. In many ways it is continuous with the thinking advocated for individual Christians in this book. But its difference is sufficiently important to deserve mention. Whereas the way of thinking discussed here aims at personal integrity, the church thought that is also needed seeks an authentic solution to a tension between the personal need for authenticity and the equally important need to work toward mutual respect among all Christians, as well as for establishing and maintaining bases for various kinds of cooperation and unity. This kind of theology must learn to use the historic language of the church to speak of the real situation of the present. It must operate at a level of generality that allows diverse interpretations while also limiting that diversity so that real guidance is given to the churches.

The tension between the need to express unity with the whole and to respond to the need of authenticity within its own life has been particularly manifest around feminist issues. Feminists have called for many and radical changes as essential to authentic Christian life and thought today. They have persuaded many members of the oldline churches, but their message has barely reached some of the churches with which these denominations try to express solidarity. A key problem arises for oldline denominations: How do they balance the need for authenticity with the need for church unity? This is another example of a problem for church theology that differs from the problems that arise in personal theology.

Church theology reacts upon the work of the individual theologian as described in this book. Church theology cannot give up concerns for unity at the denominational and the global levels that are in tension with personal authenticity. The result is that individual Christians can rarely express their full personal authenticity in the life of the community. How far can compromise go?

That is the negative formulation of the problem, and the problem it identifies cannot be evaded. But it is better first to consider a more positive response. It is possible to extend authentic personal reflection to the question of how to maintain and support community and global unity. Indeed, to fail to do this is to express individualistic assumptions that collapse when theologically examined. Hence, fully authentic Christian life and thought do not find the restrictions on personal expression, or even the necessity of taking some actions that are not satisfying, as a compromise. They are an authentic expression of the Christian faith.

But this does not solve the problem of compromise. When we believe that the actions and teachings required for corporate life and unity with the whole church cause the church to witness fundamentally *against* the meaning of Jesus Christ in our day, we must protest, oppose, and—if necessary—leave. The number who have found this necessary is considerable. Church theology has a difficult, but crucial, task to work with the tensions that have these results.